7|76
✓

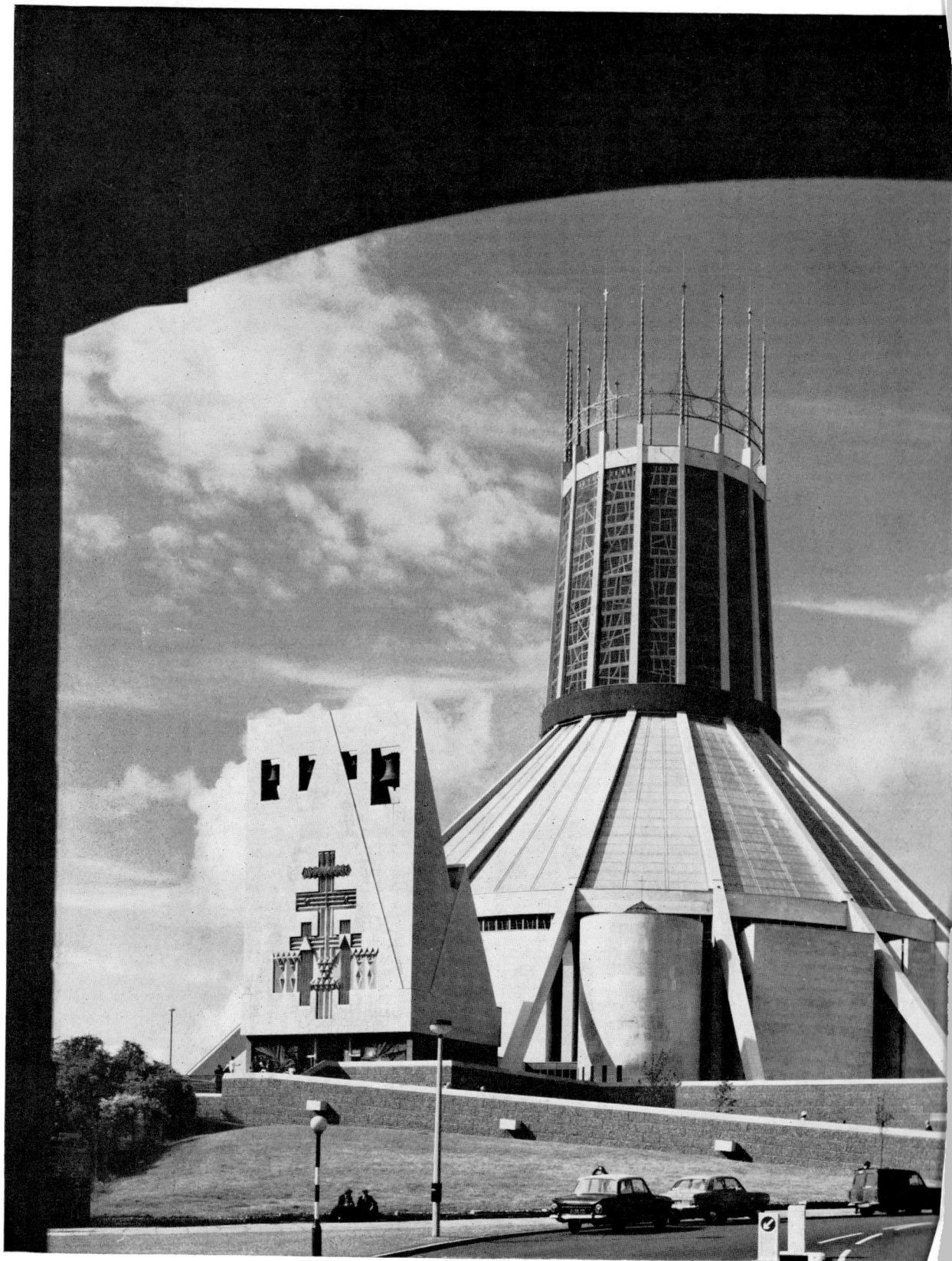

METROPOLITAN CATHEDRAL OF
CHRIST THE KING
LIVERPOOL

METROPOLITAN CATHEDRAL OF CHRIST THE KING LIVERPOOL

Frederick Gibberd

Kt CBE ARA FRIBA AMTPI FSIA FILA

WITH A FOREWORD BY HIS EMINENCE
John, Cardinal Heenan
ARCHBISHOP OF WESTMINSTER

The Architectural Press, London

85139 388 8
First published 1968
© Architectural Press 1968

Printed in Great Britain by Robert MacLehose & Co Ltd
The University Press, Glasgow

CONTENTS

5

Part four: Building the cathedral

ILLUSTRATIONS

FOREWORD

It is odd that the English city with the largest Catholic population should have been so long without a Catholic cathedral. This is no criticism of the zeal of Liverpool Catholics but, on the contrary, a tribute to their sense of values. With schools and parish churches to be built for ever increasing numbers, the expense of building a cathedral was rightly regarded as unjustified. But the time was bound to come when emerging from crippling poverty, Catholics would regard a cathedral no longer as a spiritual luxury but as an essential centre of unity and worship for the North.

The Brownlow Hill site was bought in 1930. The economic depression was lifting and there were as yet no signs of the greatest war in history which was to begin before the decade ended. Sir Edwin Lutyens designed the original cathedral for this site. He estimated its cost at £3,000,000 but the cost of a building which would not be completed in this century could hardly be estimated scientifically. When building was resumed after the war the rough estimate had multiplied ten times over. In 1955 Archbishop Godfrey, recently appointed to the see of Liverpool, authorised Mr. Adrian Scott to scale down the Lutyens design and produce a modified cathedral which though retaining the enormous dome would be much more modest in its proportions. In 1958 when I was appointed to Liverpool it was obvious that even the new project – whatever architectural merits it may have had were not in question – was too expensive. The Metropolitan Cathedral of Christ the King was thrown open to what was virtually an international competition. In theory competitors were to be citizens of the British Isles or the Commonwealth but in fact an American or Italian had no difficulty in submitting plans through a member of the Royal Institute of British Architects under whose rules the competition was held.

The book of conditions for competing architects published in October 1959 was a formidable document. Looking back it seems incredible that three hundred architects from every part of the world had the courage to attempt to comply with an almost impossible set of rules. The financial limit was one million pounds at 1959 prices. Remember this was to be a cathedral not just a large parish church. The low sum must have daunted many an architect but not the brave three hundred. Since then building costs have more than doubled. It was stipulated that the new building be wedded to the existing crypt. There must be room for 3,000 people in the body of the cathedral with an unobscured view of the high altar. It now seems that we were looking for an architect not only of talent but of genius. Re-reading the instructions to candidates it is obvious that when describing it as a challenge the promoters of the competition were not using fanciful language. In their defence it must be said that challenge was not then a vogue word.

It is interesting to read the Archbishop's letter which prefaced the book of conditions but which did not itself form part of them. It was an easy letter to write but it must have been daunting to read:

". . . Not only by reason of its majestic beauty but because it has already cost over half-a-million pounds the crypt must not be abandoned. In some way it will have to be incorporated in the new cathedral. That is your task. While free to design a building in any style, you must allow easy access between the crypt and the main building. If the crypt were virtually a half-built cathedral you might well be disheartened. But the crypt is mainly underground. It does not preclude an entirely new and distinctive design. Regard the crypt, therefore, not as an obstacle but as a challenge. The future use of the crypt need not pre-occupy you. The conditions make it clear that the siting of the high altar is for you to decide. The crypt, therefore, may be beneath it, as in existing cathedrals, or at the opposite end. The high altar is the central feature of every Catholic church. It must be the focus of the new building. The trend of the liturgy is to associate the congregation ever more closely with the celebrant of the Mass. The ministers at the altar should not be remote figures. They must be in sight of the people with whom they offer the sacrifice."

Looking at the new cathedral we see how completely Frederick Gibberd interpreted the spirit of the letter. This goes on to say "Holy Mass is the great mystery of faith. The high altar is not an ornament to embellish the cathedral building. The cathedral, on the contrary, is built to enshrine the altar of sacrifice. The attention of all who enter should be arrested and held by the altar." As you enter the cathedral you must ask yourself if the architect has understood the function of a Catholic cathedral. The glorious light coming from the mighty tower may be the first striking feature but the light itself is focussed and poured down upon the altar itself. It is the altar more than anything else in the whole cathedral which captures the mind and directs our thoughts to the great act of worship which the cathedral is built to provide.

Architects were assured that the assessors appointed to judge the competition would not do so in the light of any preconceived but undisclosed ideas. Otherwise no busy architect would have entered the competition. We did not say whether we wanted a cathedral in a modern or traditional style. Architects were simply asked to provide a building of great beauty at a small price. The condition which really set a problem was that the Lutyens' crypt must not be neglected. The layman may not know that in a competition of this kind the judges are just as much bound by the conditions as the competitors. For this reason in addition to the judges a quantity surveyor and an engineer were appointed to make sure the winning plans fulfilled the material conditions before the award was announced.

The judging of the competition took less than half the time we had set aside. The assessors were able swiftly to isolate about twenty sets of plans which were clearly of the first quality. Among them the Gibberd design (which had, of course, only a number not a name) began to emerge more and more clearly and indisputably as the winner. It is my belief that the prayers of the people of Liverpool were more responsible for the winning

design than the assessors or, for all we know, than the architect himself. I am merely repeating what the letter to competitors said in 1959. With those same words I conclude this preface:

"the priests and people of the archdiocese of Liverpool will beg God to enlighten you. You will also have the powerful prayers of our children. It is for them and their children's children that you will build. May Christ the King inspire you to create a cathedral church worthy of His Holy Name."

✠ JOHN CARD. HEENAN
Archbishop of Westminster

January, 1967.

INTRODUCTION

The purpose of this book is to describe the design of Liverpool Metropolitan Cathedral, its characteristic features, works of art and so on and to explain how they came about from the original programme, or brief, to the final consecration. There are, of course, guides to the cathedral and innumerable articles have been written about it; but they are either very generalised, or very specialised, so it seemed worth putting on record a full description of the building. In that sense it is a guide to the cathedral and, in as much as I am the one person responsible for its design and execution, it ought to be the most authoritative and the most accurate guide.

In writing this book, however, I have had a more fundamental purpose than describing an individual building: I have tried to widen the appreciation of architecture by showing how a building is designed. While there is an almost complete indifference to the art of architecture in this country, I am encouraged by the thought that many people will buy a book on a cathedral who would not dream of buying one on architecture – there is an opportunity to reach the unconverted.

I take the reader behind the scenes and show how the design of a building developed from the job it had to do, its function – for example, how new liturgical requirements were responsible for the plan form; to show how the place in which the building is erected influences the design – the tower is the complement of that of the Anglican cathedral; and, thirdly, to explain how the way the building was constructed profoundly influences its form – the flying buttresses are a solution to particular structural problems. I want, further, to show how these three determinants of form – function, environment and construction – react on each other and how they may be welded into a unified composition.

Architecture is an art, imagination or feeling enters into the making of it and, of all buildings, a cathedral is expected to be the most imaginative in conception. In the last resort the aesthetic value of the building depends on the imagination of the architect. I have tried to explain why I made the design decisions I did about function, environment and construction but, since intuition enters into so much of the design, some of my reasoning may be retrospective. I have, too, stopped short of attempting to reveal any subconscious motives, albeit I suspect my publishers would have welcomed a more revealing story of the human situation.

There is no stage in the creation of a building when it can be said that design stops and some other process takes over, and so I take my description to the final completion. It may be disconcerting to discover pictures of a giant tower crane along with those of a painted reredos, but both were fundamental to the design; in fact, one of the most fascinating aspects of the creation of the cathedral was that there was only one culture – we found ourselves in a world no longer divided between science and art.

3. Facing page: the choreographed Drama of the Mass was part of the opening celebrations

12

And how many of us there were, for the days are over when one man, an architect, could design a building and another man, the building contractor, could carry it out. All kinds of specialists were involved in the making of the building and I have tried to deal with their contributions as they affected the design. I cannot do justice to all, but at least everyone concerned is on record in the last chapter.

As with the great mediaeval cathedrals, a spirit of adventure permeated the construction of the building and there were considerable innovations. Herein lies a difficulty with this book for, whereas I have no desire to involve the reader in a specialist subject like building construction, I must try to explain it sufficiently to show its effect on the design – just as a description of a Gothic cathedral would be incomplete without an explanation of the purpose of stone vaulting.

I have aimed at explaining the wholeness of the design; instead, therefore, of dealing with special problems like acoustics or stained glass in tidy categories, I have regarded them as an integral part of the total problem.

The subject about which this book is written may, for all I know, be an indifferent work of art, but the labour of writing is rewarding, if only because it places on record an accurate story of the making of the cathedral; it will be even more rewarding if, by showing how a building is designed, it leads to a deeper understanding of architecture.

I am indebted to James Lowe for advice on the description of the structure and to my partner, Jack Forrest, for his untiring help. Raymond Philp, of the Architectural Press, has again proved a friend and mentor in the production of the book and Cluny Gillies, of the same publishers, not only did the page layouts but improved the text by his critical wisdom.

Nearly all the drawings were prepared in my office to explain the design and many of the photographs were specially taken for that purpose. Photographs were supplied by the following: Architectural Press 87 (photo. W. J. Toomey). Cement and Concrete Association 38, 39, 106, 109. Clayton Bros 58. Reg. Cox 3. Elsam Mann and Cooper 1, 4, 20, 21, 59, 60, 82, 84. English Counties Periodicals 61, 83. Fox Photos 32, 49. Lowe and Rodin 33. John Mills 2, 5, 10, 42, 63, 78. Ness Studios 16. *The Observer* (photo Ray Green) 28. F. Osborne & Co (photo Graphion) 85. Professor R. D. Russell 66. Stone Masonry (NW) Ltd (photo Stewart Bale) 75. Taylor Woodrow Services Ltd., 51, 102, 104, 107, 110. All other photographs were taken by Henk Snoek. Thanks are also due to publishers named in footnotes, for permission to quote from their books.

1. CATHEDRAL DESIGN

The cathedral as an art form

Man's belief in a divine power or powers, has been responsible for his most impressive and individual buildings; the temples of ancient civilisations like the Egyptian and Assyrian; the temples of India or China; the mosques of Islam; or the churches of Christianity: no matter where we look or how far back we go in history, the story is the same; faith produces the finest architecture.

In spite of the fantastic material progress of western civilisation, the cathedral is still the major architectural achievement. From Helsinki in the north to Seville in the south, the great multitude of cathedrals are not rivalled by any other type of building: the castle, the palace, the college, the town hall, have all produced great architecture but, compared with the cathedral, these buildings are never so alive with aspiration, never so staggering in their invention, never so charged with feeling and never so universal in their appeal.

The cathedral is the major visual expression of nearly two thousand years of culture and the more vital Christian belief was to that culture, the greater was the building achievement. Consider that almost miraculous spate of cathedral building in the twelfth and thirteenth centuries, each striving to outdo the other in the daring of its structure, the magnificence of its sculpture, the brilliance of its painted glass. Is there a greater, a more integrated work of art than Chartres? None, unless it be Albi, or Wells, or Strasbourg; the choice will inevitably be a cathedral.

A cathedral, containing as it does the *cathedra*, or bishop's throne, is the principal church of his diocese. The great cathedrals of history were the spiritual, cultural and social centres for a growing urban population – as distinct from the immense churches of the self-contained abbeys. Their function has been eloquently expressed by Marcel Aubert*

"The ancient temple was made only for the god; the cathedral is made for all. Vast, high, protected by its vaults, amply lit, it shelters all its children who come there to hide, to seek reassurance or information. It houses the magnificent liturgical ceremonies, sumptuous processions, religious dramas, assembled confraternities, corporations and popular feasts, while the echoing reverberations of the organ, and the Gregorian chants which 'modulate the silence as Gothic art moulds the shadows' (Rodin) leap upwards and rise to the summit in luminous spirals. The cathedral also gives shelter to the dead; their remains are crowded, layer on layer, beneath the paving."

A cathedral is fundamentally a simple building type: although the traditional cathedral form is a long building, subdivided into nave for

* Marcel Aubert, *Gothic Cathedrals of France*, Kaye and Ward Ltd., 1959.

laity, choir for clergy and a sanctuary beyond, and although other spaces are associated with it, like the transepts, chapels and baptistery, it is fundamentally one vast enclosed space for Christian worship. Vastness is the characteristic of the space: Amiens could accommodate nearly 10,000 people, the total population of the mediaeval city and, whereas today the congregation may have shrunk to six hundred or so, it is unthinkable that the building should shrink with it.

The cathedral is the visible expression of man's belief in God: the space and the forms that enclose it are expected to be the most perfect that it is possible to devise. It may be that today the functional solution to the problem of relating a group of Christians to an altar is a simple and comparatively small, unadorned space but such a building would not be a cathedral, as that word is commonly understood. Whether the cathedral is still a valid building type and whether its popular image of being a monument to the glory of God and a shrine for ecclesiastical art are relevant today is not for me, a nonconformist, to question. However, it is to be observed that over a million people have visited Coventry since its consecration in 1962, and at the great services that took place in the Catholic crypt of Liverpool, closed-circuit television was the nearest the majority of the congregation got to the sanctuary.

The art of architecture finds its highest expression in the art of enclosing space and nowhere is this spatial enclosure more sublime than in the cathedral. A cathedral is one vast space enclosed by a thin shell or envelope. "There are two basic elements: space and the material used to enclose it. For a work of art to emerge from the process it is essential that these two basic elements should produce a unified effect. It is not enough that the space alone should be effective; and it is not enough that the envelope enclosing the space should be effective. The art is in the effective synthesis of these two elements."*

There is a fundamental problem in cathedral design: it is that so much depends on the imagination of the designer. Unlike the majority of buildings, in which different kinds of rooms give varied spatial arrangements, everything hinges on the creation of a single major space with a few secondary ones to support it. Moreover, the building's function does not automatically produce interesting and individual forms as it does, say, in the case of a power station with its boiler house, turbine hall and cooling towers. The spires of Lichfield are quite useless structures, they serve no practical purpose: they are symbols of man's belief in a spiritual life.

Almost everything depends on the imagination or intuition of the architect. Therein lies the danger. Designing a cathedral is a perilous process for it is all too easy to fall back on obvious symbolism, to echo familiar cathedral forms like the pointed arch, to 'exploit' modern structural shapes like the concrete shell vault, or to make an 'architectural statement' by mere novelty.

Because the visual image of a cathedral is so important, some people believe that an architect sets about designing by sketching at random on

* Herbert Read, *The Origins of Form in Art*, Thames & Hudson, 1965.

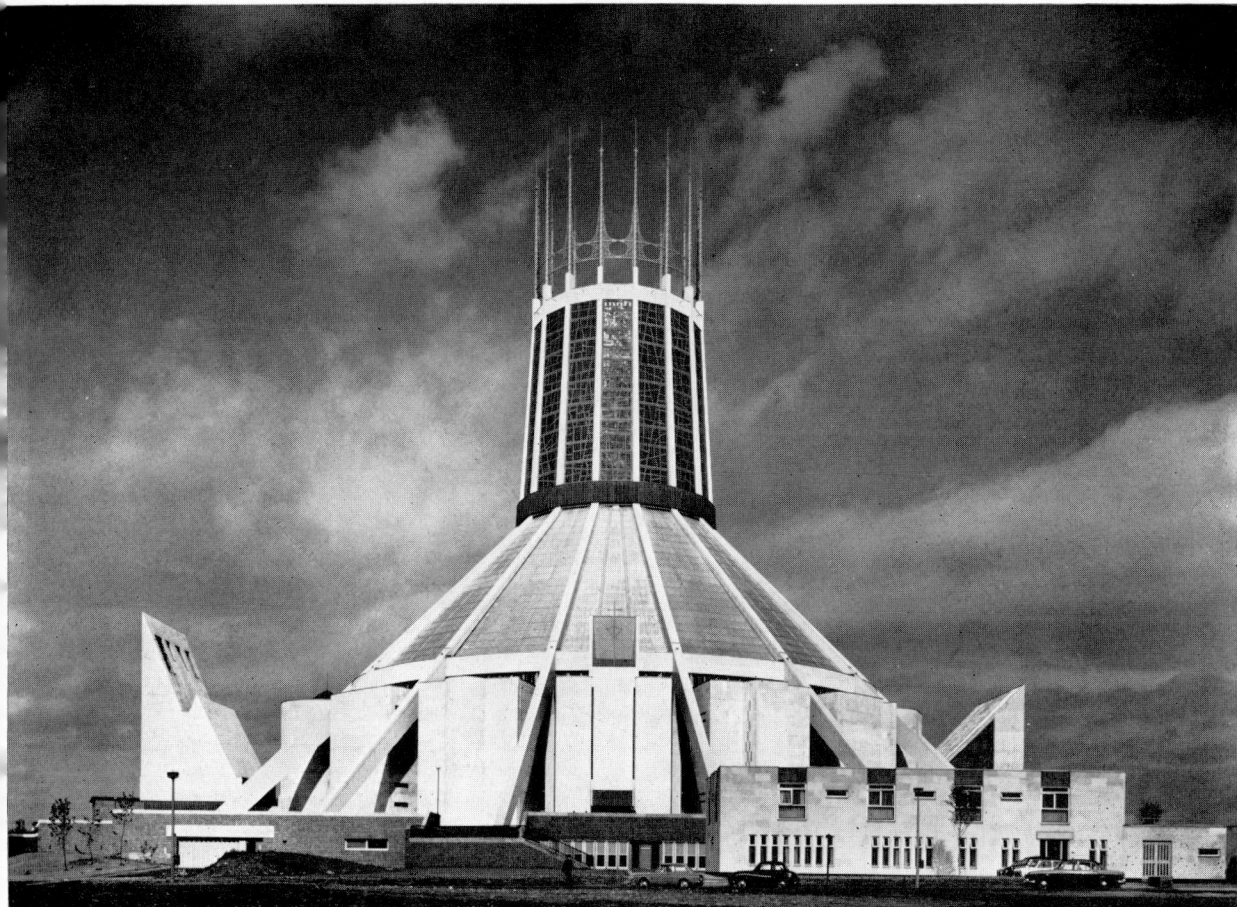

paper until he gets an inspiration; that design is evolved through a series of drawings and perspective sketches of what it will look like. Architecture does not happen in this way: if some aspect of beauty – grace, charm, austerity, monumentality, is pursued for its own sake – the result is likely to be banal or, at the best, meaningless innovation. The design of a building is a strict, laborious and long discipline; there are no short cuts to a successful solution and moments of inspiration are few.

The four determinants of form

The nucleus of the design process is function; until someone wants to enclose space for the purpose of controlling climate and giving degrees of privacy and safety, there is nothing to be designed. There is, in the first place, no distinction between the approach to the design of a cathedral or, say, a hospital, for both have the prime purpose of creating an artificial environment and neither will be entirely successful unless they function properly – which is not to say that 'form follows function', or that architecture is merely the formal expression of a building's purpose.

There are other determinants. A building is a construction; its form will also derive from the choice of materials and the way they are put together.

4. View from the east: presbytery buildings in foreground

17

5. *The city's new skyline*

And the structural system is itself influenced by such factors as the geological and climatic conditions, the type of labour available and the cost.

A building does not exist in a vacuum, it is a part of a wider environment which influences it and on which the building itself exerts an influence. Whilst its designer may delude himself that his work of art is so great that it will have an independent existence, no one else will see it so, for architecture cannot be isolated, as sculpture may be in the setting of a gallery. The recognition in the design of the character of the environment is the third major influence on form.

The ultimate determinant lies within the personality of the designer, the architect. It is his task to produce a unified work of art which communicates his feeling about the nature of the building. He will solve the functional and constructional problems by analysis and synthesis and, in doing so, will exercise his intellect; but reason is not enough, for only if the solution is fired with imagination, only if the architect uses his intuition, can the building become a work of art. A building can be designed and, indeed, it often is, by a junior draughtsman, who selects components from a catalogue and arranges them to imitate an accepted prototype; but it is unlikely to be a high order of architecture: still less if a machine like a computer is substituted for the aesthetic sensibility of a man.

The architect may choose to stress one particular determinant of form but he cannot afford to ignore the others. For example, he might attempt to find a new expression for a system of precast concrete structural wall units but, if they were responsible for the windows being badly placed for the proper functioning of the rooms, or for a violent discord with the building's environment, the result could not be an entirely satisfactory solution to the problems raised by the design. He may easily become so

18

involved with the external forms, their mass, scale or proportion, the sculptural qualities of the building, that the way they are composed no longer expresses the internal spaces. He may, more dangerous still, become so obsessed with formal expression that it becomes the sole design objective. A quite new 'architectural statement', a new 'formal experience' may, with certain building types, be a desirable objective, but only in terms of the purpose for which the building is being erected, the way it is to be built and the place in which it is to occur.

There is no ultimate in architectural expression and much depends on the nature of the building. Every building is a subject for conveying aesthetic experience but this is not to say that it must be a highly original work of art. Thousands of buildings are but components of a wider scene, the townscape: they are, for the most part, building types which have been developed from original solutions into an established vernacular: the design problem is primarily one of their relationship to the environment, not of the architectural expression of their individuality.

There are exceptions and one of these, by its nature, is a cathedral. It is expected to be an original work of art but, as I shall try to show in this book, not at the expense of function, construction and environment. Neither is it to be assumed that, because aesthetic expression is so important, design rests solely on the intuition of one individual designer. When the demand is for an original work he will most certainly be responsible for the conception, the building will be in his handwriting, so to speak: but today, with the bewildering number of new techniques and materials, he will be dependent on an ever-growing number of specialists. There is no stage at which it can be said that design stops and some other process takes place: everyone is involved, all the time.

2. THE FUNCTIONAL DETERMINANTS

The design brief

Design begins with an analysis of the functions the building has to perform and the possible solutions to them, through planning. Before this, therefore, someone must set down on paper a clear and precise programme or brief, saying for what purposes the building is to be erected, how they imagine it will be used, the amount of floor space required and so on.

Most large buildings today are so complex and the design problems they set are so specialised that the average building developer, or the client, finds it difficult if not impossible to prepare a complete and final brief which the architect can translate into the form of a building. Moreover, those who write the brief see the problem in terms of their own speciality – an operating theatre designed to the requirements of a prima donna surgeon may be unusable for his successor. It is obvious that the designer should be involved in the preparation of the brief, for he will bring to it the detached and analytical mind with which his training and experience has equipped him. Herein lies a difficulty with architectural competitions. Although the assessor must be an architect, or architects must predominate if there is a panel of judges, and their experience will ensure that the brief is a workable one, the architect competing has no direct contact with the client. The difficulty is to some extent surmounted by competitors being allowed to ask written questions during the competition period and the answers being circulated to everyone – the classic example is "Should the typists' pool have a diving board?", to which the assessor replied, "Left to the discretion of competitors".

Written questions are no substitute for a round table discussion and, were the initial brief all the contact the architect could have with his client, the competition system would not have succeeded as it has. But it is not, for the competition design determines a broad conception which must be followed by many months of detail design, during which time there can be complete *rapport* between client and architect.

It is seldom understood to what an important extent the design process can modify the brief. When they are allowed to proceed together there will emerge all kinds of unforeseen potentialities, the exploration of which may reveal new ways of using the building and these, in turn, may spark off better architectual solutions. This was our experience at Liverpool.

The conditions of the competition formed the initial brief at Liverpool. Therein were clearly set out such basic requirements as seating for 3,000,* a Chapel of the Blessed Sacrament, a Lady Chapel, about eight side chapels and a Baptistery. The sacristies were specified and provision had to be made for a choir, an organ, confessionals and bells. Other requirements were set which I will come to in due course and what to me was of

* Subsequently reduced to 2,000.

great significance was Cardinal Heenan's letter to the competitors, which he mentions in his foreword to this book.

After the competition there followed a year in which the brief and the design were developed between the Cathedral Committee and myself. And this is only part of the story, for there was the collaboration of the professional consultants, to say nothing of artists and technicians. The design and the brief grew together, like parts of a living organism.

The planning solution

The solution to the functional problems posed by the brief is sought through planning; this creative process begins with drawing diagrams and plans on a drawing board.* These plans are horizontal sections through the building, showing the sizes of the different rooms, their relationship to each other and the routes for moving from one room to another (circulation). The plan is an exact two-dimensional pattern, not a vague diagram of intentions. This building planning process is unique and it is unfortunate that there is no special word for it, for anyone can plan but only the architect is the building planner – from his first term in a school of architecture until his final thesis in the fifth year, the architectural student is being trained to plan buildings. No other technician is so trained.

It is from the flat, two-dimensional plan on the drawing board that the building grows into a three-dimensional space that can be walked about in. Everything develops from the plan and so the aim is to produce a plan of order, equilibrium and clarity. For, if the inside of the building has these qualities the outside may have them too, but if the plan is weak, indecisive or woolly, the appearance of the building will almost certainly have these attributes.

When an architect is drawing plans he is, of course, using his aesthetic sensibility. He is visualising the quality of the spaces formed by the lines which represent the walls: what it is really like to be in the rooms which are shown diagrammatically in horizontal section. He determines the heights of the spaces by diagrammatic vertical sections through the building. These two types of drawing – plan and section – give him a complete picture of the spatial qualities of the building. From the plan and section he sets up diagrams (elevations) of the exterior of the building. From these three types of flat drawing board diagram – plan, section and elevation – he has a complete mental picture of what the building will be like from inside as a space and what it will look like from the outside as a mass. He may make perspective sketches or models to help him visualise the appearance, but no other information is really required for the complete realisation of the building, other than specifications of the type and quality of the materials; it is only a matter of elaborating on these drawings, to show to a larger scale the details of the construction.

* In architecture the word 'planning' does not stand for the loose and much-abused word used to describe the attempts of technologists and politicians to control future events; neither does it mean the continuous, adaptive and often restrictive process of town planning.

The design process is not, of course, a tidy one of considering plan, section and elevation in that order. The internal volume and the external mass grow in the mind simultaneously and often fragmentarily; but this must be the sequence if one accepts that function is the basis of architectural design.

To me the most significant part of the brief was Cardinal Heenan's letter. In it he said, "The high altar is the central feature of every Catholic church. It must be the focus of the new building. The trend of the liturgy is to associate the congregation ever more closely with the celebrant of the Mass. The ministers at the altar should not be remote figures. They must be in sight of the people with whom they offer the sacrifice. . . . Holy Mass is the great mystery of faith. The high altar is not an ornament to embellish the cathedral building. The cathedral, on the contrary, is built to enshrine the altar of sacrifice."

The obvious solution seemed to be a centralised plan with the congregation grouped round a circular sanctuary in the manner of a Greek theatre (6).* On this pattern it was possible to place 2,000 people within 80 ft. of the sanctuary steps. Through the influence of the environmental conditions, which I shall come to, the plan devised was a circular one but it is not centralised in practice, for there is no seating behind the altar and this, with the rectangular form of the altar itself, gives direction to the building.

In so far as the seating is concerned, the plan could just as well have been a semi-circle; what is of importance is that the circular form is a natural grouping in which the people have a sense of physical proximity both to the activities in the sanctuary and to each other, which latter emphasises the communal aspect of worship.

This is not to say that the circular plan is the ideal type for a modern Catholic cathedral; as the Reverend Peter Hammond rather acidly said in a broadcast on the competition, "Long, thin churches are out and round churches with central altars are now the fashion". Forms such as the square, the octagon and the ellipse are just as valid, but at Liverpool, when other factors were also considered, the circular form seemed the answer.

Although the rectangular altar and the seating give orientation to the plan, they are not sufficient to counteract the tendency of a circular form to pivot on itself. This lack of direction was overcome by forming a strong north to south axis through the centre of the building: the main entrance porch was placed at one end and the most important chapel, the Chapel of the Blessed Sacrament, at the other end, behind the altar. At right angles to this principal axis a secondary one is formed by east and west entrance porches: in other words, a Latin cross is superimposed on a circle.

The liturgical significance of the Chapel of the Blessed Sacrament is underlined by its position as the termination of the main axis and its relationship to the sanctuary by the clear view provided between their respective altars.

The choir was placed behind the altar in the space between the sanctuary

* Numbers in brackets refer to numbered illustrations.

and the Chapel of the Blessed Sacrament and the organ in a gallery over the entrance to the latter. With this arrangement the choir have a clear view of the sanctuary (they themselves are worshippers) and all sound comes to the congregation from the same source; the organ itself has a position of prominence worthy of its unique form and one which reinforces the main axis without coming into conflict with the sanctuary (6).

In the competition design the nave floor was dished to give everyone a clear view of the sanctuary but this was later abandoned at the wish of the Cathedral Committee, on the grounds that it was too characteristic of an auditorium: a decision that was undoubtedly right for, apart from any association of ideas, the uninterrupted view puts individual members of the congregation in a position of being spectators of the liturgy rather than active participants.

6. *The main elements of the cathedral's plan. The primary axis is indicated by the horizontal line, the secondary axis by the vertical one*

Key: 1. Sanctuary
2. Chapel of the Blessed Sacrament
3. Choir
4. Organ
5. Baptistery
6. Porches

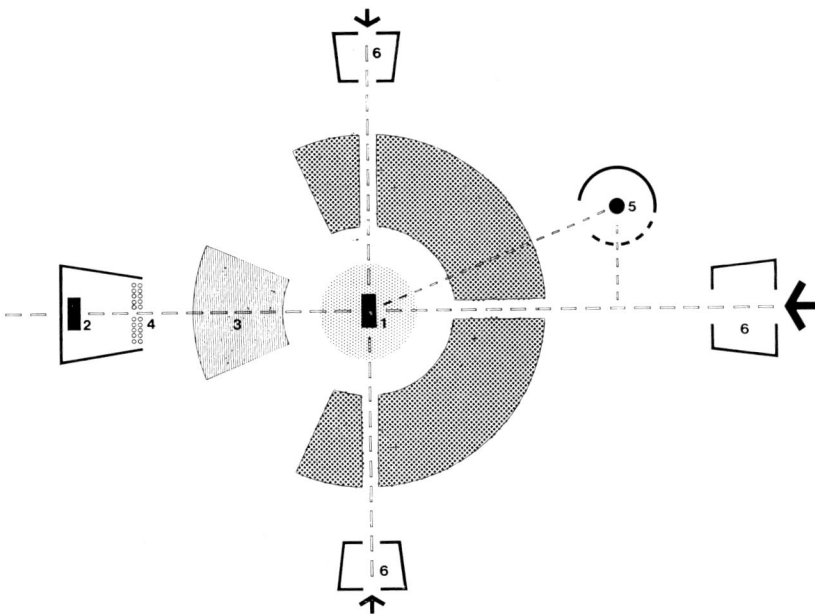

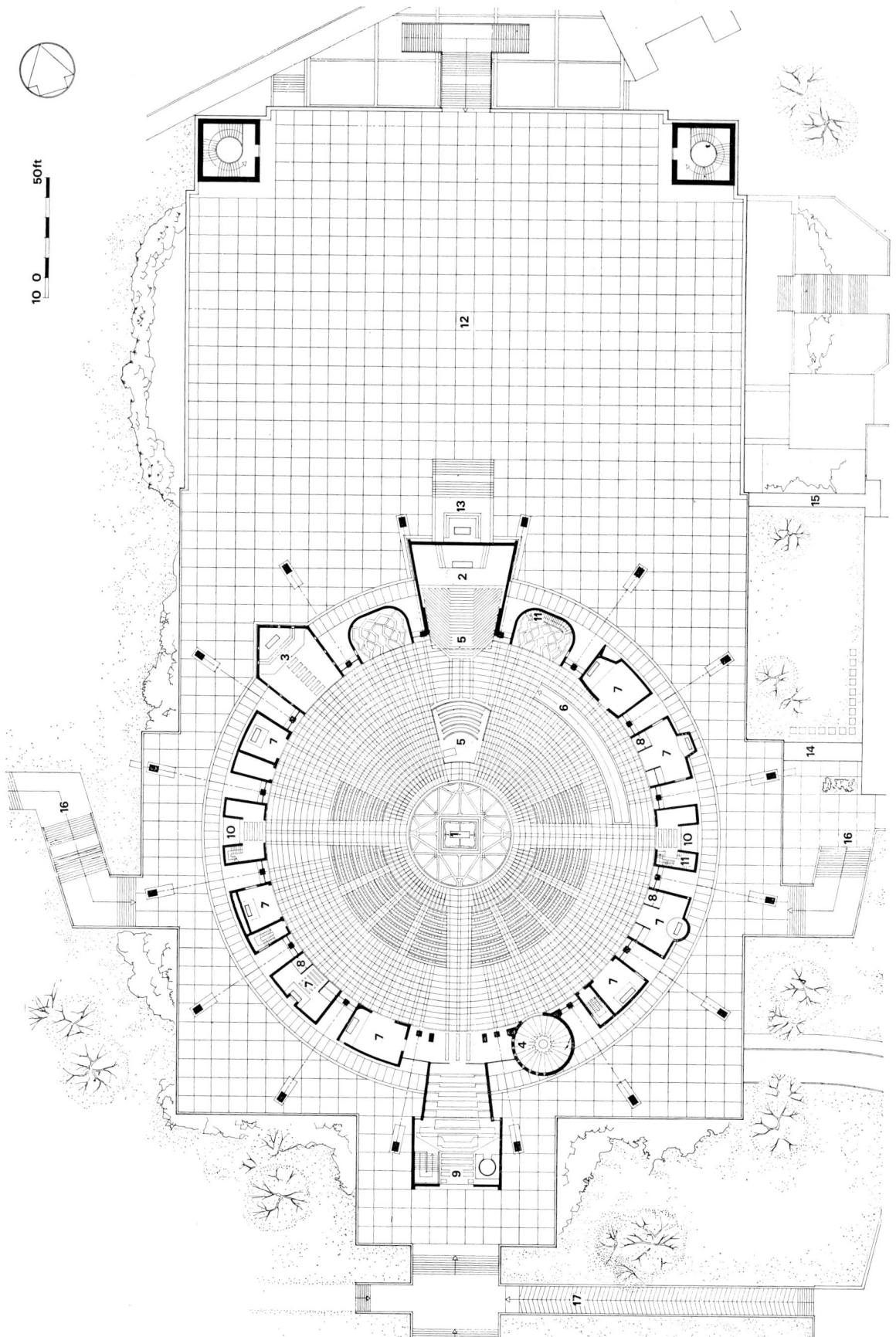

50ft

10 0

7. *Facing page: plan at ground floor level: nave and podium*

Key: 1. Sanctuary
2. Blessed sacrament chapel
3. Lady chapel
4. Baptistery
5. Choir and organ
6. Ramp from sacristy
7. Side chapels
8. Confessionals
9. Main entrance porch and bell tower
10. East and west porches
11. Stair to sacristy
12. Roof of Lutyens crypt
13. External altar
14. Link to presbytery
15. Link to convent
16. Stair to street level
17. Ramp to street level

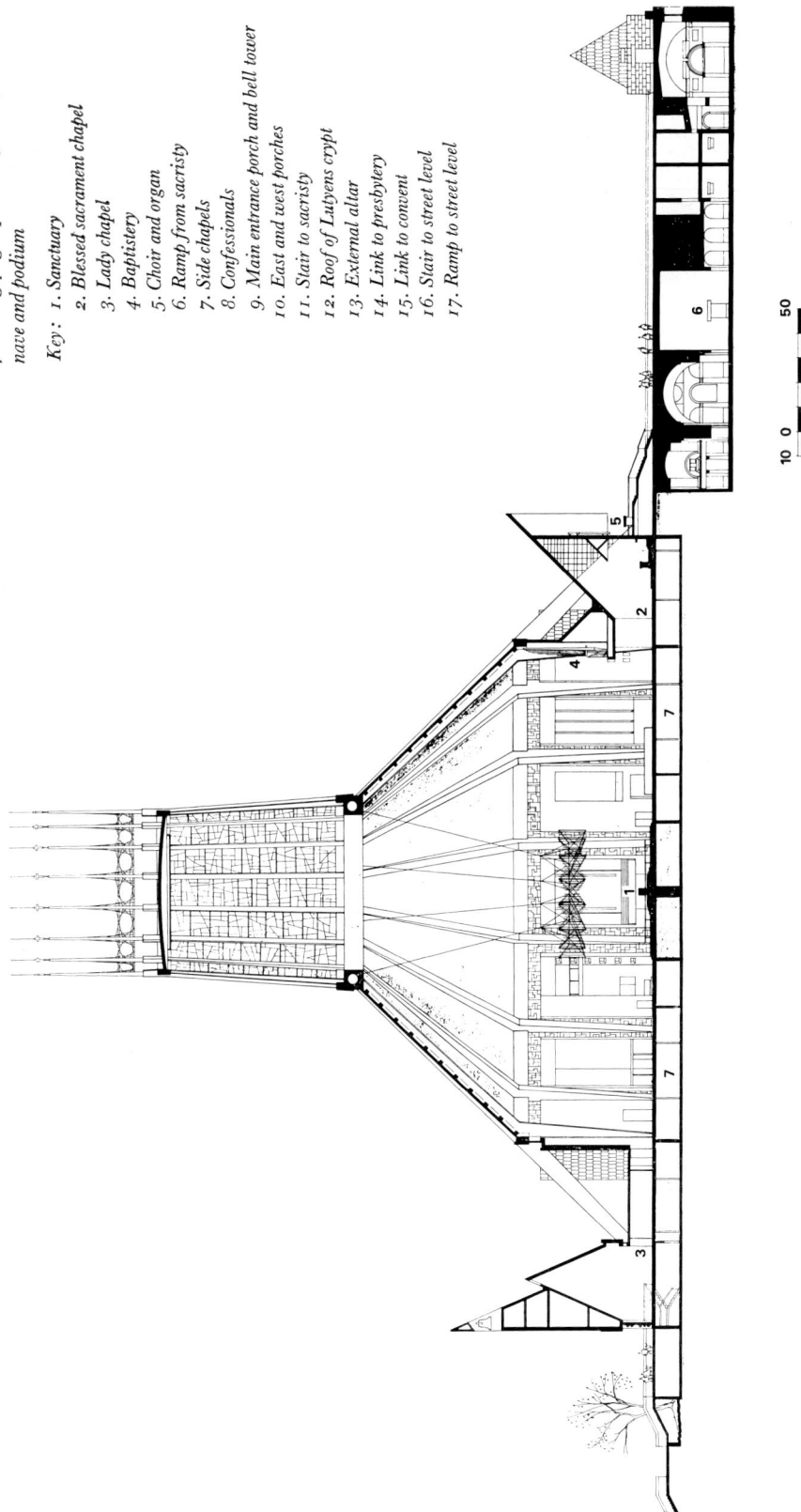

8. *This page: longitudinal section. Entrance porch at left, the Lutyens crypt is at the right. Scale in feet*

Key: 1. Sanctuary   2. Blessed Sacrament chapel   3. Entrance porch and bell tower   4. Organ   5. External altar   6. Lutyens crypt   7. Car park

10 0   50

25

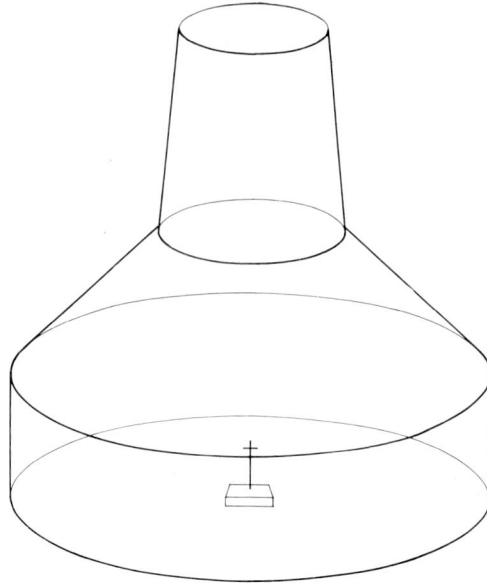

9. The nave space, in which a cylinder is developed by a conical roof, into a tapering tower

Evolution of nave space

In considering the development of this plan form to a space or volume it seemed to me that, if the sanctuary was to have its maximum expression the greatest space should be over it. Therefore, the circular plan became a cylinder, which was the nave, the cylinder developed into a conical roof and the cone extended upwards in the form of a tapering cylindrical tower (9). In this way the most significant space is over the most significant religious place, the sanctuary. Unlike the mediaeval cathedral, where the tower marks the crossing between the nave and transepts, the tower at Liverpool is an extension of the sanctuary.

It would have been a simpler solution by far to have left the roof as a cone or, for that matter, put a thin concrete saucer dome over the nave; but how poverty-stricken this would have seemed compared with, say, the towers of Canterbury, Durham or York, to name but a few of those splendid symbols; besides, there was also the challenge of Sir Giles Gilbert Scott's Anglican cathedral only a short distance away.

A building composed of curved planes can be difficult and costly to construct and so I adjusted the circular plan to a polygon, the sixteen sides of which, although straight, meet at such an obtuse angle that the form is little removed from a circle. At the junction of the planes I envisaged reinforced concrete trusses which would extend from the ground to the top of the building to form a frame holding together the walls, the roof and the tower.

There was thus a building in the form of a continuous space, and held together by a continuous frame: and one, moreover, in which not only is the internal space exactly reflected by the external form and silhouette but the most significant internal space, the sanctuary, is expressed by the most conspicuous external form, the tower.

10. Facing page: the small buildings stand between the sixteen trusses of the structural frame. The rectangular podium extends (top of picture) over the existing crypt

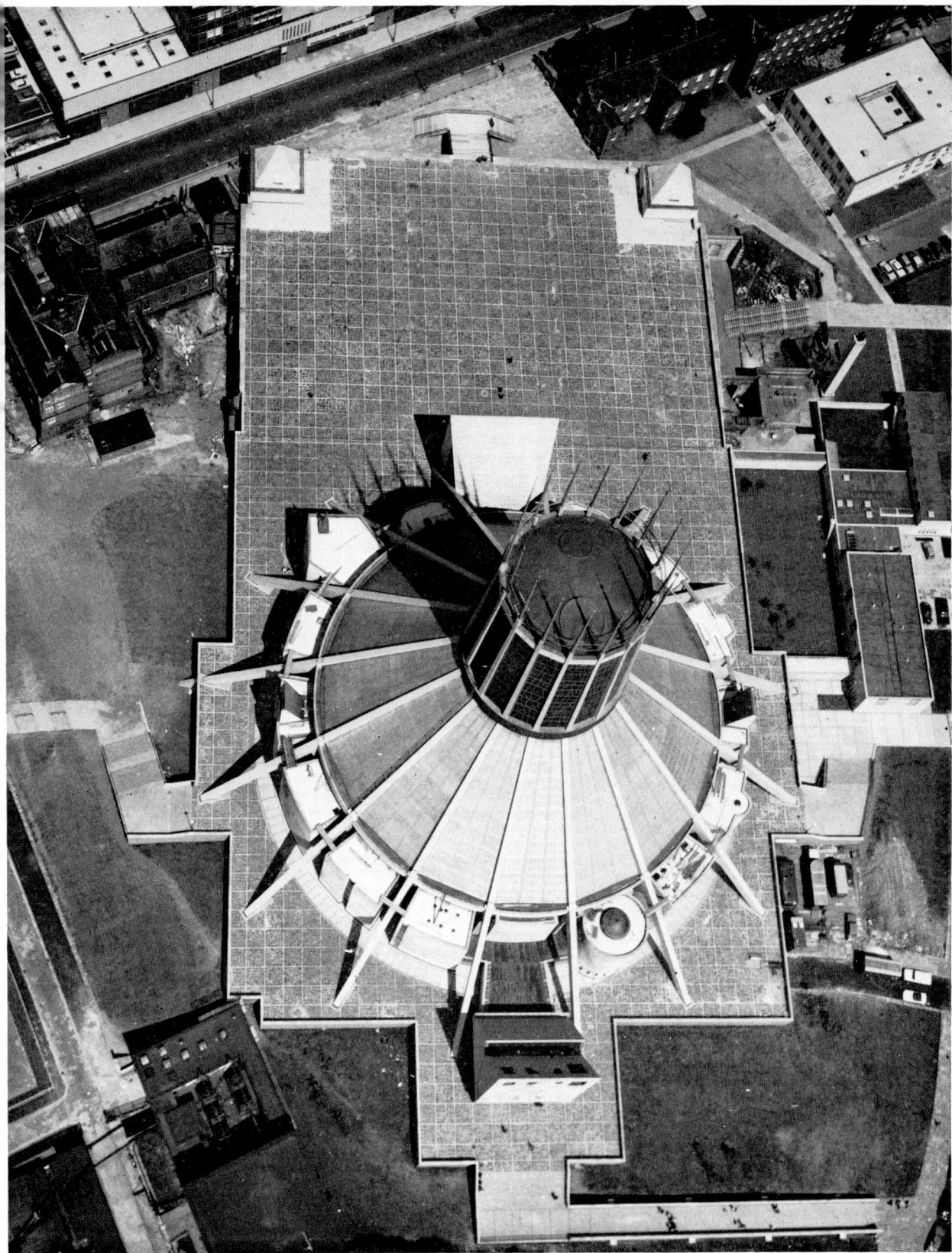

As the focus of the internal space is the sanctuary, it required the highest intensity of lighting which suggested that the tower should be glazed, to provide the main source of natural light. The simplest solution was to fill the space between the main structural ribs with glass held in a metal frame, as I had, in fact, done in the spire of a small chapel at Hopwood Hall, near Manchester: but it seemed that so large an area of glass would contrast so strongly with the conical roof and walls below, that the idea of a total form and space would be jeopardised. I therefore envisaged thick coloured glass set in a pattern of concrete ribs: the glass to flood the sanctuary with a diffused coloured light, the concrete to merge with the main frame as a homogeneous form: a tower in this form would be reminiscent of the solid mediaeval tower but extended in function to become the method of lighting the heart of the building.

As I at no time envisaged the building as a transparent or translucent one of glass stretched over a structural frame, it seemed that a similar glass and concrete technique should be used in the nave walls; but only of sufficient area to provide reasonable reading conditions to the perimeter spaces, leaving the heart as the highest intensity.

The sixteen independent buildings

The conditions of the competition asked for eight side chapels as well as a Lady Chapel and the Chapel of the Blessed Sacrament. Although small chapels are often fitted into odd corners, cathedral designers have shown innumerable other ways of disposing of them: from projecting them outwards, as in the radiating apses of French Gothic cathedrals, to hollowing out spaces within the structure, as in the elaborate geometric patterns of Baroque churches.

The problem of providing these small spaces seemed at first a difficult one. My desire was to provide one decisive major space, having geometric proportions and formed by a clear and articulate structure. It seemed that the introduction of small spaces could only confuse these objectives. The idea came to me (by intuition: the reasoning is retrospective), that each of the chapels should be complete in itself as an independent design, which could stand in the spaces between the main structural frame. If to them were added the other small individual buildings, like the baptistery and porches, all sixteen perimeter spaces would then be filled (10). The buildings thus take the place of walls and, in order that both their shape and that of the structure should be crystal clear, they are separated from the frame by bands of coloured glass. The glass infilling forms a method of lighting the perimeter of the nave; that above the chapels being in the form of a continuous clerestory, and that at the sides a series of vertical windows.

The sixteen individual buildings form the walls of the nave and are not used to admit natural light to the rest of the interior, which enables each to have window openings only sufficient for its particular needs. Furthermore, since they are independent buildings, they are not involved in the structural mechanics of the main frame, again freeing them as individual designs. The design of each building could thus be developed from its

11. From a distance the chapels merge to become the walls of the cathedral

12. Near to, each takes on an identity of its own

*13. From some viewpoints the buttresses merely
disappear between the solid perimeter buildings*

*14. Facing page : from other viewpoints, they
stretch upwards to the tower and pinnacles*

30

function, making possible considerable spatial variety between each other and between each one and the nave space – some could be opened up as an extension of the nave, others shut in as secluded rooms.

The small chapels and the east and west porches are of similar outline with their outer perimeter wall struck from the same radius. Three other small buildings, the circular baptistery and the two elliptical staircases to the crypt, are contained within the perimeter radius, but the Lady Chapel and the Chapel of the Blessed Sacrament project well out to provide the floor area required and to mark their importance; and the main entrance porch leaves the cathedral altogether, to become a free-standing structure with a low linking porch.

There is thus the external effect of sixteen solid buildings placed as free-standing elements between the soaring structure of the cathedral: seen close to, each one has an identity of its own (11) but from a distance they merge to become the walls of the cathedral (12). There is considerable interplay of form between the structural frame, the glass and the buildings themselves which gives a wide diversity of external appearance, depending on the view points and the lighting conditions. At the one extreme, as when the buildings are seen in three dimensions, there is an appearance of great solidity and mass (13); at the other there can be the dynamic effect of the structure, as when the frame is seen extending upwards to the tower (14). There was, of course, the danger that the diversity in design between the individual buildings would lead to a chaotic appearance but the scale of the cathedral and, in particular, the broad expanse of the roof cone and the powerful forms of the structural frame, appear to me to hold them together as a unity.

The geometric basis

I have explained how the purpose of the building and the desire for a tower produced a circular plan form. But it is possible that my classic training inclined me towards the opportunity to use a perfect geometric figure, the circle – the basis of so many Renaissance ideal town and building forms. Be that as it may, most building design is based on Euclidean geometry, for the simple reason that, by and large, rectangular rooms are more convenient to use than irregular ones, apart, of course, from the difficult problems that arise with the manufacture of buildings of free flowing form – for example, they are almost impossible to depict as intelligible diagrams and they inhibit the use of machines in construction or fabrication. Architects who discard the right angle in the interests of self-expression seldom find that their designs come to fruition, for, even with a plastic material like concrete, the moulds into which it is poured have to be drawn and constructed: Gaudi and Rudolf Steiner are rare phenomena.

Once a geometric basis for the design was accepted there was the possibility of adopting some system of numerical proportion. I went no further than making the dimensions multiples of a module. A module, or unit of length, assists in the manufacture and assembly of buildings (with prefabricated systems it is essential), and, although, in a 'one-off' design like Liverpool, this is of no great importance, the module is useful as a design discipline. For example, a building in which the dimensions are multiples of, say, a metre, is likely to have more overall unity than one based on a centimetre.

The size of the cathedral is largely determined by its seating capacity and, since the congregation is arranged concentrically round the sanctuary, the obvious dimension to take for a basic module was the distance apart of the seats from back to back, namely, 3 ft. 0 in.

The diagram (15) shows the module applied to the building. On plan the sanctuary is eighteen modules in diameter (54 ft.), the adjacent aisle four modules and from there the plan expands outwards in concentric circles, based on modular dimensions, to its total diameter of seventy-nine modules, or 237 ft. The same discipline was imposed on the heights but, in places, it was relaxed to enable costly structural members, like the main ring beam, to be the absolute minimum size. The figures in the diagram are to the nearest module and, whereas the total modular height is $89\frac{1}{2}$, or 268 ft. 6 in., in actual fact the height is 268 ft. 5 in.

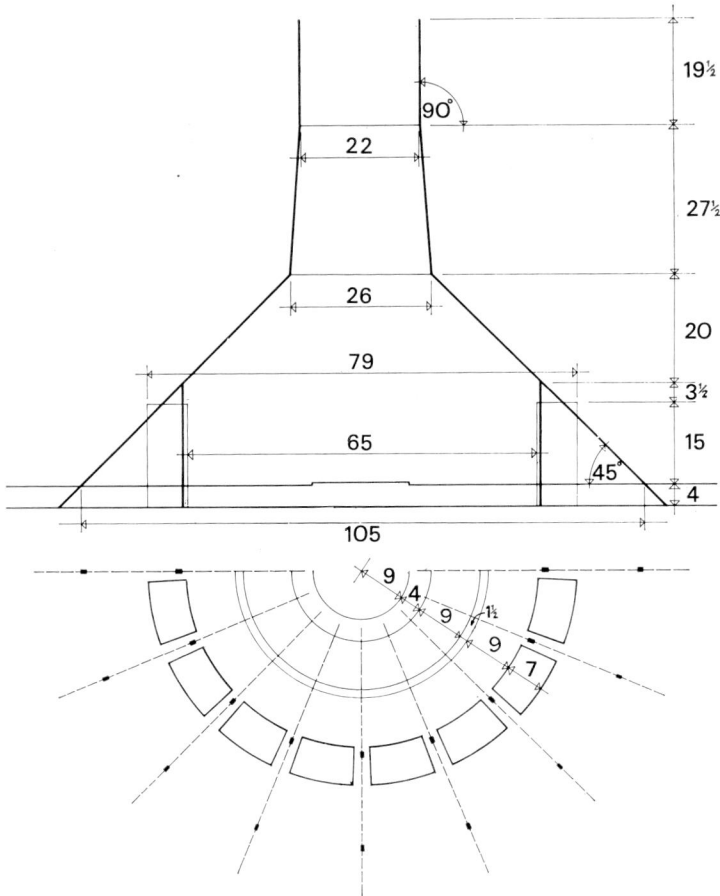

15. The building measured in 3 ft modules

3. THE ENVIRONMENTAL DETERMINANTS

Character of the place

The design, as it has so far emerged as a solution to the functional problems posed by the brief, is an abstract artefact: it exists in a vacuum, so to speak. But while it was being evolved there was always the site on Brownlow Hill asserting its influence; the design was never, in fact, a self-contained form, having no identity with the place it was to occupy.

Few sites in the built-up centre of a great city could be better suited for a cathedral precinct. Situated on high ground, dominating but contiguous with the city centre in the river valley, there was no fear of it becoming aloof, either as a monument or as a part of the social organism. Being bounded on the north and east by the new university precinct, on the west by catholic schools and on the south by the inner city, there are no conflicting building uses, no fear that the site would become completely shut in by buildings, and every opportunity to provide an ambience proper to a great cathedral.

At the time of the competition the site had an air of dereliction (16): surrounded by outworn housing, untidy building sites of the new university precinct and broad assertive roads; the only topographical features of any character were the red brick Gothic university tower and the Catholic diocesan offices on Brownlow Hill. Moreover, those were the days before Shankland, Cox and Associates had prepared a plan for the city centre and showed how the cathedral could be related to the business and civic zones; above all, how the precinct, with the university, could become part of an environmental area (that is, a unified area – free of through traffic).

The site plan provided with the conditions of the competition is shown opposite (17). The southern end was cleared of buildings except for two squat and ugly nuclear physics buildings erected by the university under a

16. The site before construction began; the rectangular Lutyens crypt is nearing completion

lease from the Catholic Diocese – who later regretted it. As the principal frontage of the site, and opposite the long vista down Hope Street, they form a disastrous introduction to the Catholic precinct from the heart of the city. At the north end, immediately behind the diocesan offices, was the huge rectangle of the Lutyens crypt, rising some twelve feet above ground level, in a litter of contractor's plant and hoardings. There seemed nothing here that should influence the character of the new building except, perhaps, the quality of the ground itself: the red sandstone of the hill was revealed by old excavations and ferns grew in crevices in derelict basements.

The conditions stated that the existing buildings would one day be swept away and that the new cathedral could be anywhere on the site, providing it was linked to the crypt; the only restriction was that the main entrance had to be from the southern, city centre end.

The cathedral as crown

Most buildings are but parts of a wider scene, the town itself; they are elements which require to serve the broader composition of the town's spaces – that this is so seldom recognised in a civilisation that measures designs in terms of novelty, is the main reason for the squalid appearance of so many town centres. There are exceptions, like those buildings which, by reason of their special function and importance to the town's organism, may dominate the scene; and of these, the cathedral, being an expression of man's belief in God, can be the most dominant, just as a palace of culture or sport might be the focus in a community of atheists.

The great cathedrals of Christendom are generally the crowns of the urban composition. What a fine instinct for topography their builders had when they chose spectacular sites like Durham or Lincoln, or when they raised their buildings to dominate flat environments – the spire of Salisbury, the focus of the plain, or the dome of St. Paul's rising above the compact city mass of London: compact, that is, until it was utterly destroyed by the slabs and towers of post-war reconstruction.

At the time of the competition Liverpool already had one crown, the

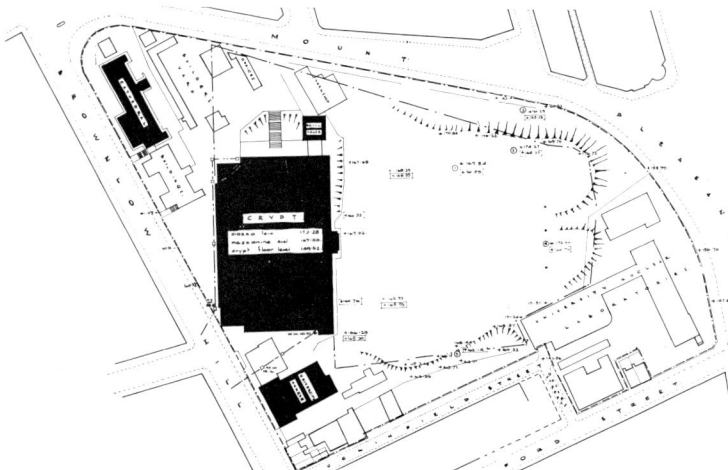

17. The site plan issued to competitors. The new cathedral has to be approached from the south, the right-hand side of the diagram

35

Anglican Cathedral, by Sir Giles Gilbert Scott, which stood on a rocky prominence some three quarters of a mile from Brownlow Hill; by happy accident, connected to it by Hope Street. There was thus an opportunity not to be missed of giving the city a unique topography of two crowns (21). Whether or not there was a case for extending the cathedral space upwards in the form of a tower, there certainly seemed one for balancing the Anglican tower with a Catholic one. Lutyens had envisaged his design for the Catholic cathedral as a monumental composition, building up to a stupendous dome which, had it been realised, would have dominated the scene and reduced the Anglican tower to insignificance – what might possibly have been a gain to architecture would most certainly have been a loss to civic design.

Scott's design is the traditional Gothic form of a massive square tower over the crossing of nave and transepts; built of dark red sandstone, it appears as a sculptural, solid block rising from a monumental substructure. The design had developed from a quite different liturgical brief from that of the Catholic cathedral; it uses different material and systems of construction and is inspired by a different aesthetic attitude. Clearly, to reflect these qualities in the new building could only result in an anachronism or, at the best, topographical scene painting: the problem, as I saw it, was how to make two quite dissimilar forms complement and balance each other across the intervening space.

So diverse and unexpected are the views of silhouetted forms in the

18, 19, 20. Facing page top, the first model of the tower; bottom, changed to a less assertive form; this page, as built

urban scene that their relationship can never be exactly calculated in advance – those responsible for introducing tower blocks into city centres have had some surprises, if not unpleasant shocks. All that can be done, apart from making drawings and studies in which the design is super-imposed on photographs of critical viewpoints, is to use one's intuition. I, for my part, began with a tall tower with a pronounced taper (18) which, as I became more familiar with the topography, changed in proportion to become less assertive, with a heavier, more cylindrical drum and less effect of upward thrust (19); and it was subsequently reduced in height and mass until it reached the final form (20).

The two towers now react on the Liverpool scene and on each other in the most diverse and often surprising ways: they can be balanced (5); more often one dominates the other (21); but at all times one is conscious that Liverpool has two crowns of equal prominence. Whether, in the course of time, this unique skyline will be destroyed by a plethora of tower blocks and slabs, rests on the civic values held by the City Fathers and their professional advisers.

38

The crypt and podium

Whatever one may feel about Lutyens' design for his cathedral, there can be no doubt that the crypt is a superb example of brick construction used on a monumental scale.

Although the competition conditions allowed the crypt to be built over, this seemed to me to be a course fraught with danger, for apart from any question of interference with Lutyens' design, let alone its use as a temporary cathedral, there could be acute foundation problems. I decided, therefore, to place the new building quite clear of the crypt on the southern end of the site; a decision for which we were all subsequently thankful as little information could be found on the construction – the story was that no accurate drawings of the structure existed because, unknown to Lutyens, the consulting engineer took the precaution of pouring concrete on top of the brick vaulting.

This decision left the difficult problem of how to handle the crypt, for its flat box-like form, projecting 12 ft. above the ground, was so dissimilar to my tall cylindrical one that a satisfactory relationship between them seemed impossible.

The solution, which in retrospect seems obvious, was to extend the roof of the crypt over the southern end of the site, doubling its area and forming a large platform or podium. The centre line of the crypt became

22. Site plan

Key:
1. Cathedral
2. Blessed Sacrament chapel
3. Main entrance porch and bell tower
4. East and west porches
5. External altar
6. Roof of Lutyens crypt
7. Ramp to street level
8. Stairs to street level
9. Stairs down to crypt
10. Service road
11. Presbytery
12. Convent
13. Chaplaincy
14. Existing office block

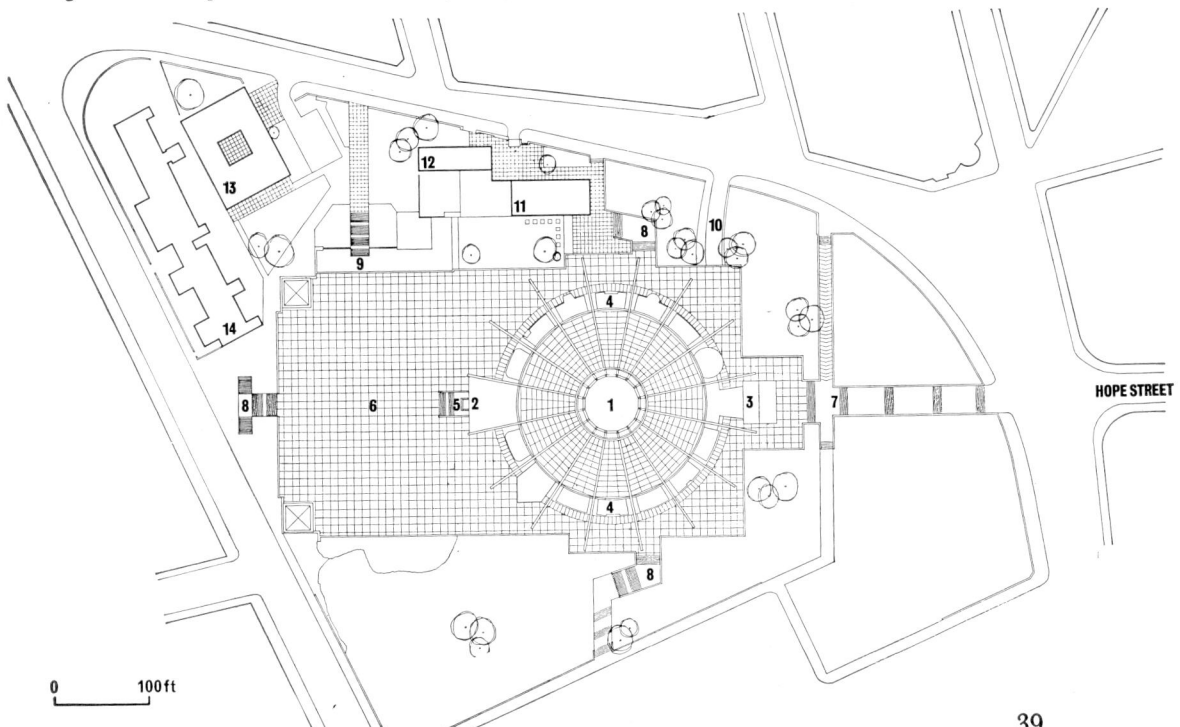

HOPE STREET

0   100 ft

39

the longitudinal axis of the new podium on which the cathedral is placed – leaving the top of the old building as a piazza. In this way the crypt became absorbed into the design for the new cathedral, the whole area being paved to form a new ground level, with no distinction between the old work and the new.

The site plan (22) shows the final arrangement: the main access to the podium is from the south; at the other end the piazza is designed for open-air services with a raised altar placed against the blank end wall of the Chapel of the Blessed Sacrament (24) and a broad flight of new stairs at the opposite end to enable crowds to disperse clear of the cathedral. As the diameter of the new building is greater than the width of the crypt, the piazza expands on the secondary axis and incorporates flights of stairs leading to the east and west porches. The ground levels surrounding the piazza were remodelled so that broad sweeps extended into steep and irregular banks against the walls of the building – the existing rock formation was, alas, too deep to be revealed.

There is thus a circular building standing on a precise rectangular base (10); the total geometric composition being imposed upon and contrasted by the irregular surroundings. The topographical value is perhaps obvious for, once a building is raised on a plateau, it gains in importance and monumentality simply through being dissociated from its immediate surroundings; it gains, too, because the base is elevated above eye level, requiring the spectator to look up at all its forms, (24) – it was for these reasons that the architects of Greece or Rome raised their most important building, the temple, on a stylobate or podium. Moreover, new views are released outwards, from the podium itself, looking over the surroundings; these can include dramatic contrasts between precise forms in the foreground and distant irregular skylines (25).

Two-level planning

This environmental determinant had an immediate impact on the functional solution, for raising the building released the existing ground and made it possible to plan on two levels. Town planners have discovered that some form of two-level development is inevitable in shopping centres if the conflicts between the motor car and the pedestrian are to be overcome, and whilst traffic problems on the cathedral site were not likely to be critical, the possibility now arose of obtaining complete vehicular-pedestrian segregation.

The two-level system is explained by the cut-away drawing (26) and the lower ground floor plan, (27), is also shown overleaf. A road passes through the building from side to side at the southern end, giving access to a parking garage and service bays below the nave and an entrance porch under the main porch and bell tower. The road is designed so that cars can draw up before the lower porch from which a staircase and lift lead to the main porch and cathedral entrance above. An internal road encircles the building, with the cars ranged in a tidy pattern round a solid inner core under the sanctuary. The spaces between this parking garage and the rectangular perimeter are utilised as stores for chairs, candles and mechanical and other equipment. This two-level planning enables the piazza and its approaches to be exclusively pedestrian; it enables the motorist and the infirm to have direct access to the cathedral under cover and it clears the site of unpleasant car parks.

In the competition design the sacristies were placed on the piazza in the form of a small building linked by a covered way to the nave. As this would interrupt the free flow of pedestrians round the cathedral and spoiled the clarity of the plan, I subsequently lowered the accommodation to the floor below, with a ramped processional approach to the nave – so unusual a method of leading the clergy into the nave was too risky a proposal to have suggested for the competition.

26. Cut-away drawing

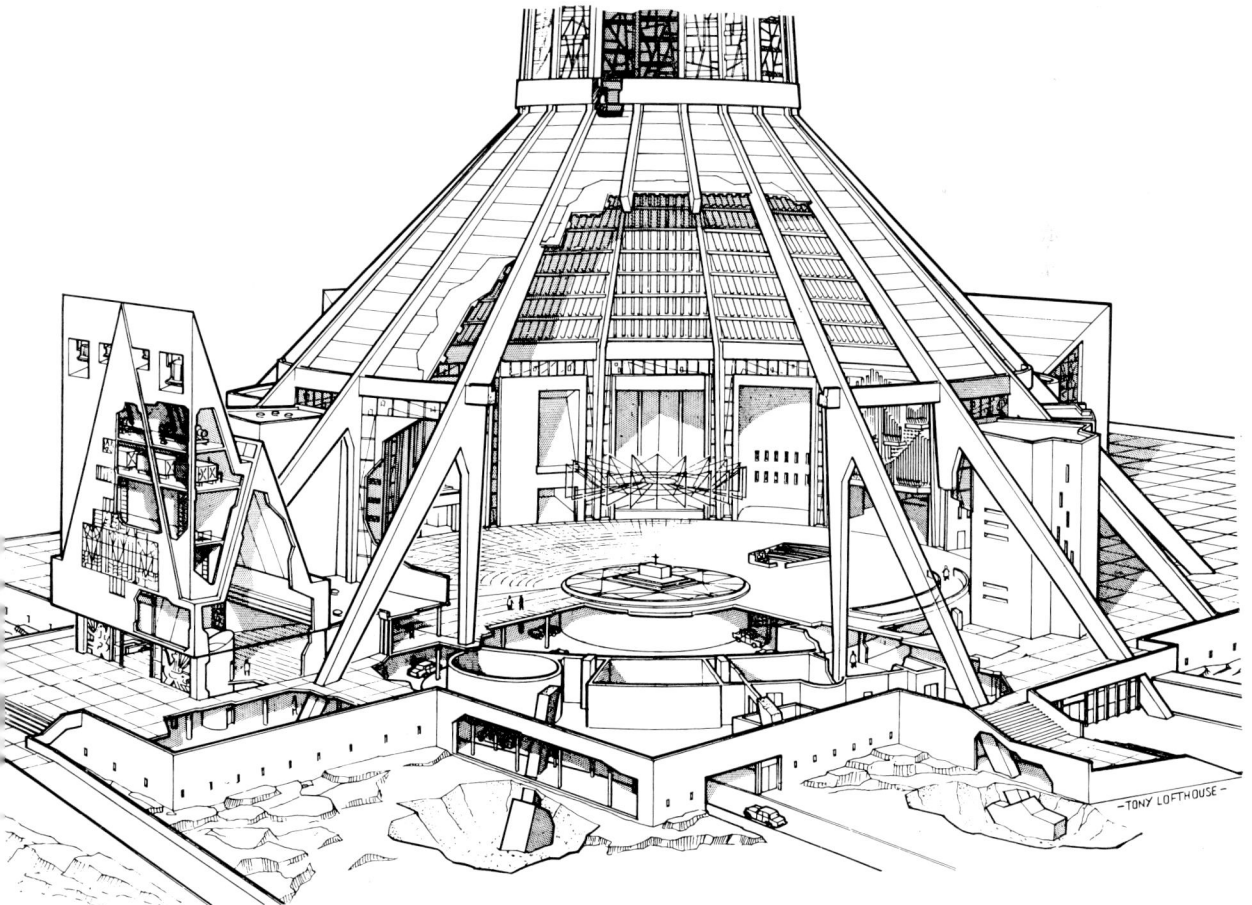

-TONY LOFTHOUSE-

The sacristies are ranged, with natural lighting, against the east side of the podium, on either side of an external entrance porch on the secondary axis. The sacristies are linked by a wide 'forming-up' area, where the priests and choir boys assemble before they climb the segmental ramp to emerge into the nave and process to the sanctuary.

The ramped approaches

The raised ground level gave importance to the views of the cathedral; it also made possible a whole series of controlled and unfolding view points from the ramps and staircases between the old and new ground levels.

Large crowds of people will, on special occasions, arrive at the cathedral forecourt and it seemed to me that a long ramp would be a far less laborious method of climbing the 25 feet to the main entrance porch than a flight of stairs. There was, too, the problem of formal visits by ecclesiastical or other dignitaries; approach by motorcar to the lift and stair in the lower porch cannot be seen and so they are more likely to be set down in the forecourt and then climb under the eyes of the crowd up to the cathedral doors; for this, a ramp is obviously preferable to the jerky climb of a stair. The competition design therefore proposed a ramp of monumental proportions thrusting forward on the main axis of the cathedral from the main porch towards the city centre. When, later, it became clear that the temporary nuclear physics buildings that clutter up the south frontage would not be removed in time for the building operations, I designed a secondary ramp at right angles to the main axis and made corresponding reductions in the width of the main one.

The ramps are designed as solid structures growing out of the ground (see illustration on title page) and are dissociated from the podium by a flight of stairs in the form of a bridge, so that their respective forms do not become confused and so that the natural landscape may continue round the base of the cathedral.

At present only the secondary ramp exists but one day the two will give access from the south and east sides of the forecourt (with covered setting-down bays for coaches between them) and will converge on the platform in front of the main porch.

As already mentioned, staircases on the secondary axis of the cathedral lead to the east and west porches; the east staircase rises from a small forecourt on which is sited the entrance to the sacristies (4) and at the northern end is the broad flight of stairs for large crowds attending open-air services.

This system of ramps and staircases, apart from giving scale to the composition through their monumental character, provide a series of unfolding viewpoints between the lower level, where the tower of the cathedral stands out in clear-cut silhouette against the sky (4), through a series of truncated views as one ascends (23, 14), to the detailed close-ups of the nave (13), or, on turning round, open prospects of the surroundings (25).

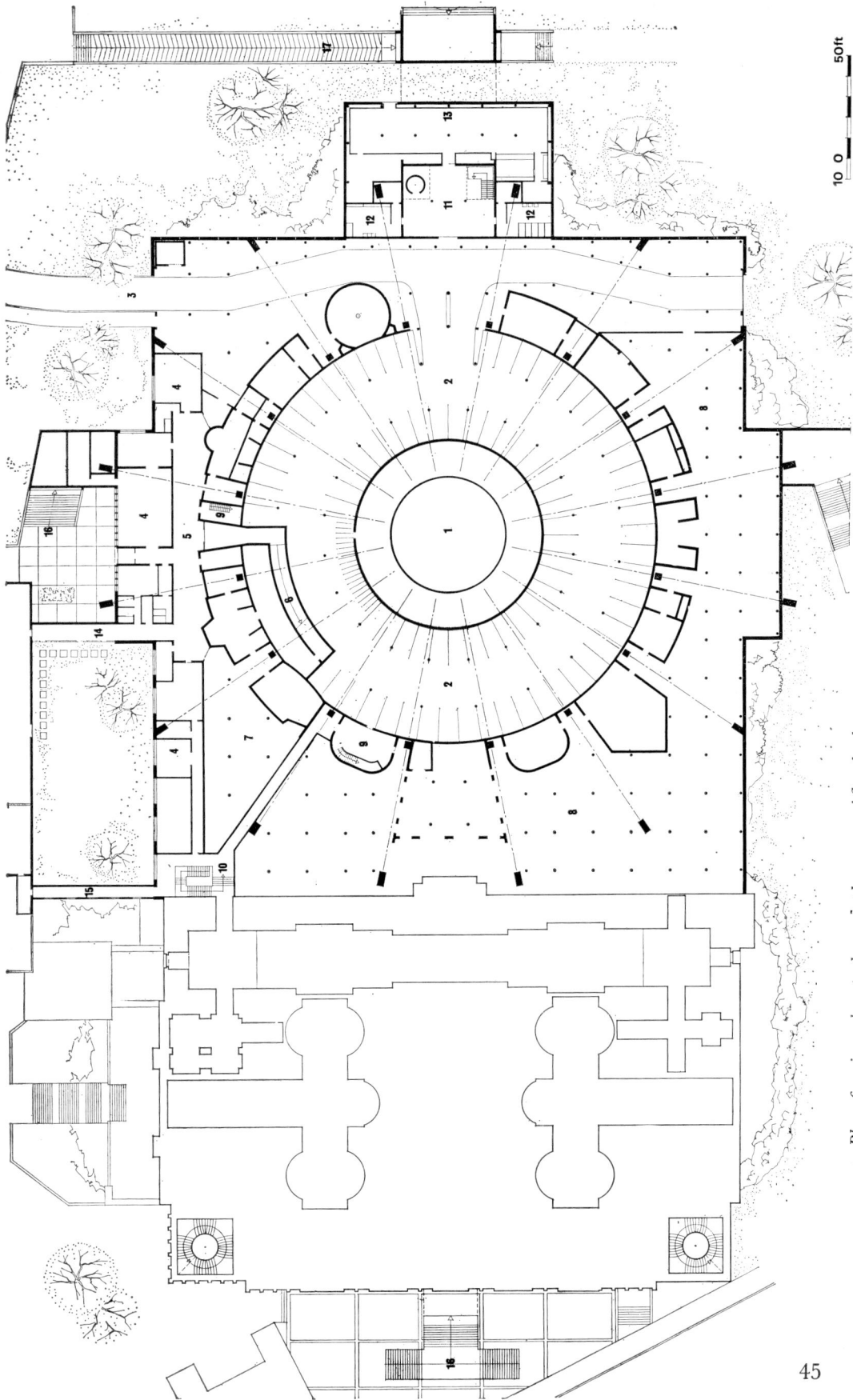

27. Plan of service and car park areas at lower ground floor level

Key:

1. Area below sanctuary
2. Parking garage

3. Service road
4. Sacristies
5. Forming-up area

6. Ramp to nave
7. Chair store
8. Storage

9. Stair to nave
10. Stair to crypt
11. Entrance porch

12. Lavatories
13. Tea room
14. Link to presbytery

15. Link to convent
16. Stair to podium
17. Ramp to podium

45

The silhouette

In the atmosphere of Liverpool there is little of the bright sun and hard, clear light that made possible the precision of form and silhouette of the classic architecture of Greece and Rome. The atmosphere tends to be diffused and ethereal; the sun, if it appears at all, struggles through a haze of clouds. It has always seemed to me that the spiky silhouette of the Gothic cathedral mingles perfectly with the atmosphere of the Gothic North; rather than leave the tower as a rigid geometric form I diffused the silhouette by a structure of pinnacles.

Each of the sixteen structural ribs of the tower is extended some sixty feet above the roof, in the form of pinnacles surmounted by crosses and spikes. To strengthen the pinnacles against the pressure of high winds, they had to be braced by diagonal members, which it seemed to me might form a symbolic crown. To surmount the Cathedral of Christ the King with a crown could be symbolism of a very obvious, even trite order, so I used the bracing against wind pressure as a design discipline, restricting the elements to only those that were structurally useful. The problem was complicated because I also wished the crown element to merge the strong verticals of the pinnacles into the cylindrical form of the tower. In the competition design I envisaged the pinnacles as being of a dull bronze with some kind of cast iron stiffening tracery between them but subsequent exploration into the structural problems* and cost resulted in black epoxy resin and concrete pinnacles with steel bracing and gilt aluminium crosses.

The pinnacle structure was an economical way of gaining height to balance the Anglican tower – the dimension from the pavement in front of the cathedral to the crosses is 282 ft., as against the 347 ft. height of the other tower above pavement level in St. James's Road.

The final design is shown in the picture opposite (28): whether it is reminiscent of a crown or not is of little importance compared with its success as a method of heightening the tower and merging its precise form with the Liverpool atmosphere.

28. The cathedral's silhouette is designed for a northern atmosphere

* See page 60.

46

4. THE STRUCTURAL DETERMINANTS

The structural challenge

Few architects living in Europe could design a cathedral without being conscious of the structural daring of the great mediaeval builders. With simple tools and primitive machinery they made fantastic structures and they made them out of stone, a material that is quite useless in tension – that is, it has to be built up block upon block, like a child's bricks. By the use of the pointed arch and a system of cross-rib vaults they raised soaring structures of an incredibly slender framework, with walls a mosaic of coloured glass and roofs a canopy of stone. They took the most terrible risks and the most terrible things happened. The Norman tower of Ely collapsed in 1322 and they replaced it, not with a safe and conservative design but a quite new conception, an octagon, which they found was too wide to vault (70 ft.) and so they invented a splendid timber structure – which, incidentally, was not, as far as I am aware, the inspiration for the Liverpool lantern.

Structures like these are a challenge to inventive genius and how much greater are the opportunities today with so many new materials, so many systems of construction and so exact a knowledge of how they will behave under stress and strain. But therein lies a danger, for so stimulating, so 'exciting', to use an expression beloved by architects, are new forms like the giant cantilever, the space frame, the hyperbolic paraboloid, that they may come to be adopted for their own sake, irrespective of the other determinants of architectural form. Structure does not exist to show how ingenious man can be. The structure is a challenge but the challenge is not to produce an imaginative structure but rather to develop a structure with imagination within a unified design. Inventiveness in structural design emerges with inventiveness of the other design factors, modifies them and is modified by them.

As I have explained, the functions the building had to perform and the environment in which it was set led to the placing of the sanctuary in the centre of a drum-like nave and extending it upwards by means of a conical roof into a tapering tower: for ease of construction the circular plan form became a polygon and the structure was developed as a cage of sixteen structural members extending from the ground to the top of the tower. Between this structural frame stood the sixteen independent buildings surrounding the nave.

Reinforced concrete

It seemed to me from the outset that reinforced concrete offered the greatest possibilities of providing a structure with significant architectural form which could both perform its task with the least possible amount of material and reflect the total unity of the space.

Pouring concrete in a mould in which steel reinforcement has already been placed, sounds a simple enough discovery, but until the invention of reinforced concrete there were only three ways of enclosing a space: the post and lintel, the arch and the dome. What an experience it must have been to discover that, when a concrete slab spans between two concrete beams, they become homogeneous and co-operate; and then to realise that, since the slab can transmit loads in any direction in its plane there need be no beams at all – only a single continuous slab.

Reinforced concrete has an extraordinary physical quality, which distinguishes it from all other materials and that is, it can be formed into almost any structurally stable shape without the application of heat. So versatile is it that within a remarkably short space of time it has given to architecture quite new structural forms like the mushroom column, the flat cantilevered slab, the thin shell roof. But perhaps its greatest visual contribution is that, for the first time, a structure can be monolithic. Every other building material needs to be assembled to form a space; but, although the joints of a reinforced concrete structure may be a structural problem, in terms of appearance they need not exist. Furthermore, unlike stone or, for that matter, almost any other building material, there can be, through the plastic quality of concrete, a form that almost exactly represents the line of stress. Nervi's astonishing series of halls at Turin and Rome have an absolute clarity of structural expression which is in itself a formal expression of the great spatial envelopes – here is the essential spirit of mediaeval building, genuinely alive again.

While all the tendencies in the design of reinforced concrete structures are towards pre-casting their parts in a factory and only assembling the finished parts on the site, I had envisaged the structural frame as a continuous in-situ structure, (in situ means moulded in one piece, on the spot), which would best express the totality of the space it enclosed. This intuitive choice coincided with the general requirement that a cathedral should have a long life: an in situ structure has no joints and so evades the critical problem in designing a pre-fabricated building, which is not the design of units themselves but how to joint them together to form a stable structure that keeps the moisture out.

Evolution of the structural frame

My first idea for the sixteen structural frames (29) was a boomerang shape, rising vertically from the foundations for the height of the nave, then sloping inwards at an angle of 45° for the roof cone and finally extending upwards again to form the tapering tower and pinnacles. Each whole frame was thus one continuous structure from the ground to the top of the tower.

D

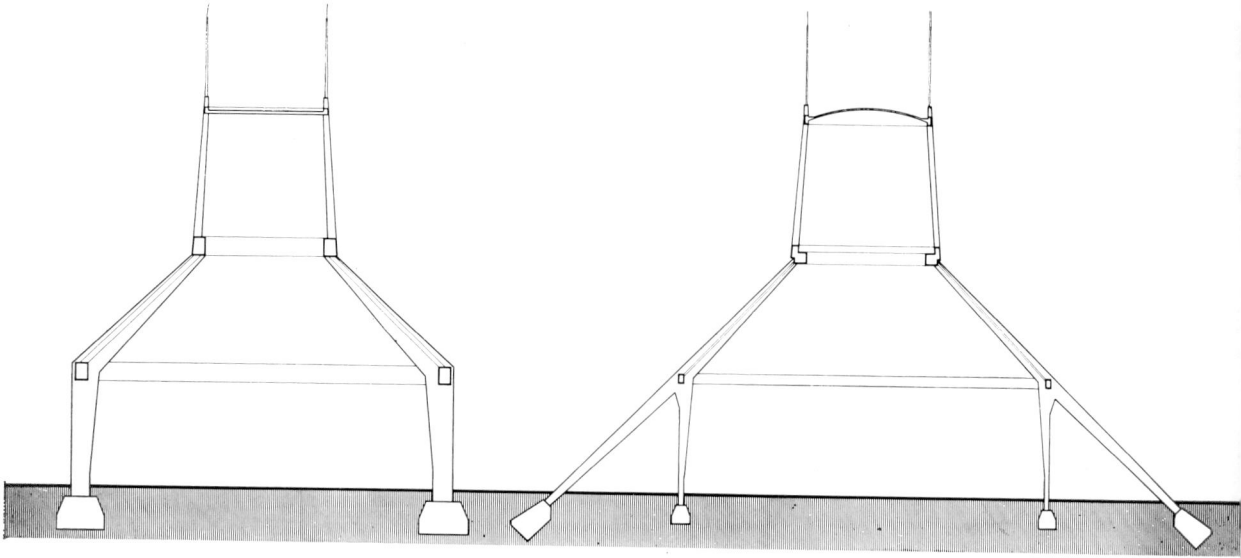

These sixteen trusses were ranged in a circle and held together by two horizontal beams (in the form of rings), where the trusses changed direction: one ring at the junction between the walls and the roof cone and the other ring at the junction of the roof cone and the tower. There was thus a rigid and continuous reinforced concrete cage carrying the loads of the building, between which would be placed the independent buildings and the non-structural infilling.

The appeal of this design to me was that the tower, unlike those of history where the weight was carried to the ground by vertical piers, is poised in space over the nave, and when filled with a blaze of coloured light, would appear to float over the sanctuary. What was less attractive was that the change in direction of the load between the roof and the walls made the frame very deep at the junction – the two arms of the boomerang would splay or curve into each other, making a clumsy knee. At this stage I sought the advice of the structural engineer, James Lowe, who suggested that the roof ribs should be carried straight down into the ground as flying buttresses (30). With this form the weight of the roof and the tower is divided over a triangulated frame consisting of the vertical nave column and the inclined buttress. The two meet together at the ring beam and the junction at this change of direction becomes relatively light and taut.

The picture opposite (31) shows the frames as actually constructed – their plastic form tapering up from the ground clearly demonstrates the lines of force and is eloquent of the extraordinary gifts that science and technology have given to the art of architecture.

I did not at first like the idea of the flying buttresses, as they appeared to make the structural expression too assertive, besides which their raking

50

31, 32. Left: the frame under construction. Right: Cardinal Heenan examines the model under test

lines trace out a section of a cone which belies the drum-like form of the nave. It was not until the stage of construction was reached, when the strong vertical walls of the perimeter buildings counteracted the diagonals, that I began to feel happy about them.

In the completed building there is, as I have said, considerable interplay between the soaring forms of the structural ribs and the static mass of the buildings standing between them: from some view-points the frame dominates as when the buttresses appear as giant props (12); in others the frame is suppressed by the mass of the perimeter buildings (13); but, all told, I hope that the total effect is one of balance between a dynamic frame and static buildings.

The structural theory

The design of structure is now almost an exact science; so much is known about the nature of stresses in a building and so much about the qualities of building materials themselves that the economical shape and size for the structural members of most buildings can be determined mathematically. But when the design is a new and original one, intuition will have entered into the conception and when, moreover, the structure is itself required to be a means of architectural expression, then it may be too complicated to

51

permit a precise analytical solution.* There can be an element of risk and so provision must be made for analysis by models. Such was the case at Liverpool where models of the frame were tested in engineering laboratories to verify the design assumptions – the picture (32) shows Cardinal Heenan with a concrete model of the frame at the Cement and Concrete Association.

James Lowe's analysis of the structure is shown on his drawing (33) opposite. Putting it very simply indeed, there are two types of load to be dealt with: vertical, which is the weight of the building; and horizontal, which is the force of the wind. The top drawing shows the complete structure with its two types of load: quite simply, the pinnacles sit on the tower, the tower sits on the conical roof, the main ring beam at the top of the cone takes the outward thrust; and all these weights are supported by the columns and buttresses of the triangular frames. The whole structure is thus more or less in compression.

The centre right diagram shows how the vertical or dead load of the building is dealt with. The weight of the pinnacles and the tower goes straight down vertically into the top of the roof cone, which is the main ring beam. The cone takes the weight of the tower and adds its own load. It is designed as a series of self-supporting circlets which partly resist the load; but that which is not resisted, the main load, goes straight down the main ribs to the lower ring beam and then through the flying buttresses and vertical columns of the nave, down to the foundations on the rock.

The bottom left diagram explains how the horizontal wind load is transmitted to the foundations. The tower is braced against wind pressure by connecting four pairs of main ribs (in a quadrant) with diagonal metal braces. The wind pressure from the pinnacles passes from the tower into the dome roof. When the wind strikes the tower, half of the load travels up to the dome roof and half down to the main ring beam. All the loads gathered in the dome travel down the pairs of braced ribs in the tower to the main ring beam. The load then travels down the cone to the level of the lower ring beam, where it is transmitted to the foundations by the sixteen triangulated frames, the leeward half being in compression and the windward half in tension.

The main frame

The main structural frame was designed to be built independently of the podium and the small buildings which would be built afterwards. The drawing overleaf (36) is a section through half of the building showing one of the sixteen frames extending from the foundations up to the top of the tower. Each of these frames, together with the ring beams at the top and the bottom of the tower, is a continuous *in situ* structure, but the pinnacles were prefabricated as they are not primarily structure members.

---

* When the structure is hidden, however, as when a steel frame is buried in a wall, all kinds of expedients, of which no one will ever be aware, can be employed to ensure that the structure is safe.

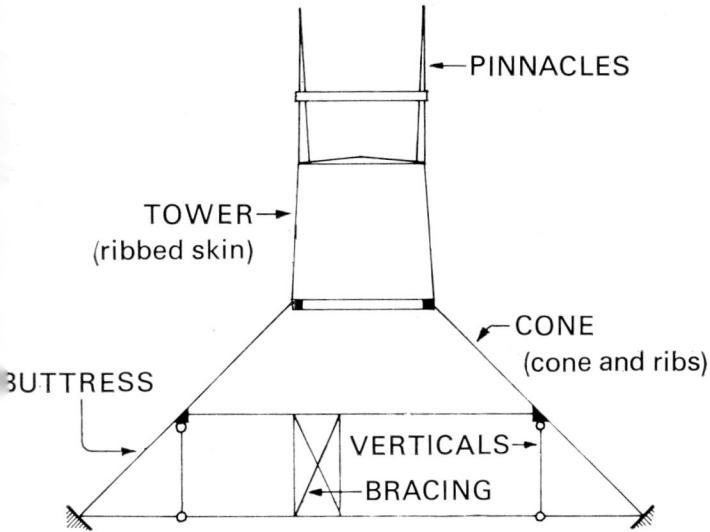

PINNACLES

TOWER
(ribbed skin)

CONE
(cone and ribs)

BUTTRESS

VERTICALS

BRACING

33. Structural conception: basic loads and their support. The structural engineer's analysis of the structure

Vertical loads: pinnacles, supported on

tower, supported on

compression ring beam and lower structure, which resists load in rib compression and cone compression

Horizontal loads: wind on pinnacles passes loads to

tower, wind is added and load passes to

lower structure which resists load by compression and tension in buttresses

53

34. *Cross-section of main ring beam,*
where the cone roof meets the tower

Key:
1. *Tower glazing*
2. *Aluminium weathering*
3. *Exposed aggregate panels*
4. *Maintenance platform*
5. *Mild steel safety balustrade*
6. *Hollow core to beam*
7. *Precast concrete purlin*
8. *Precast pre-finished cone roof panels*

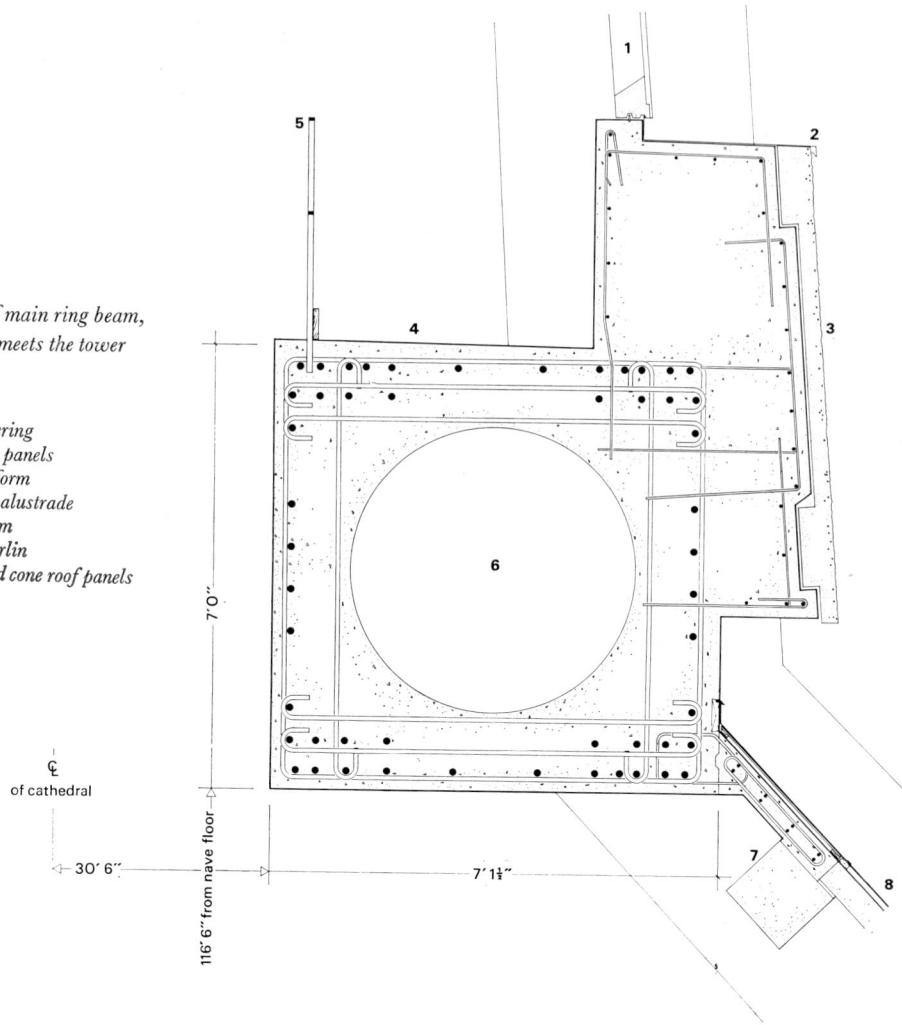

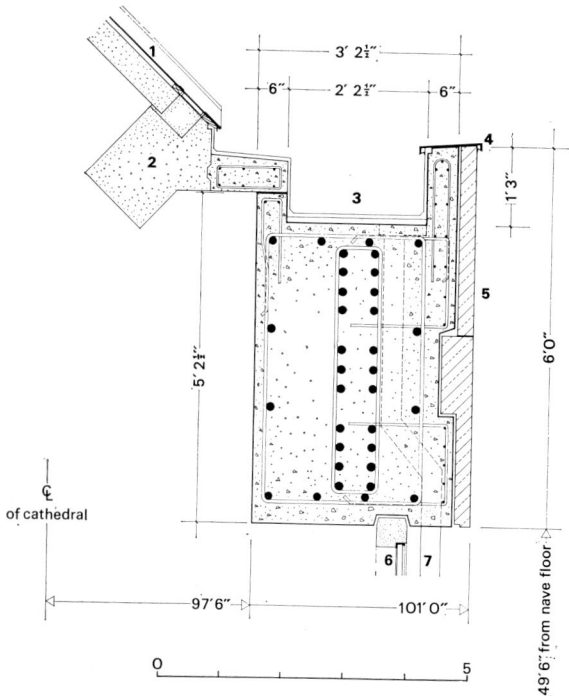

of cathedral

7' 0"

116' 6" from nave floor

30' 6"

7' 1½"

35. *Cross-section of lower ring beam,*
between the conical roof and the nave walls.
Scale in feet

Key:
1. *Precast pre-finished cone roof panels*
2. *Precast purlins*
3. *Asphalt gutter lining*
4. *Aluminium weathering*
5. *Portland stone*
6. *Nave window panels*
7. *Aluminium rain water pipe*

3' 2¼"

6"   2' 2¾"   6"

1' 3"

5' 2¼"

6' 0"

of cathedral

97' 6"

101' 0"

49' 6" from nave floor

0   5

54

52' 8"

6' 0"

Upper ring beam

5' 3"

66' 9"

257' 5"

3' 3"

Main ring beam

7' 0"

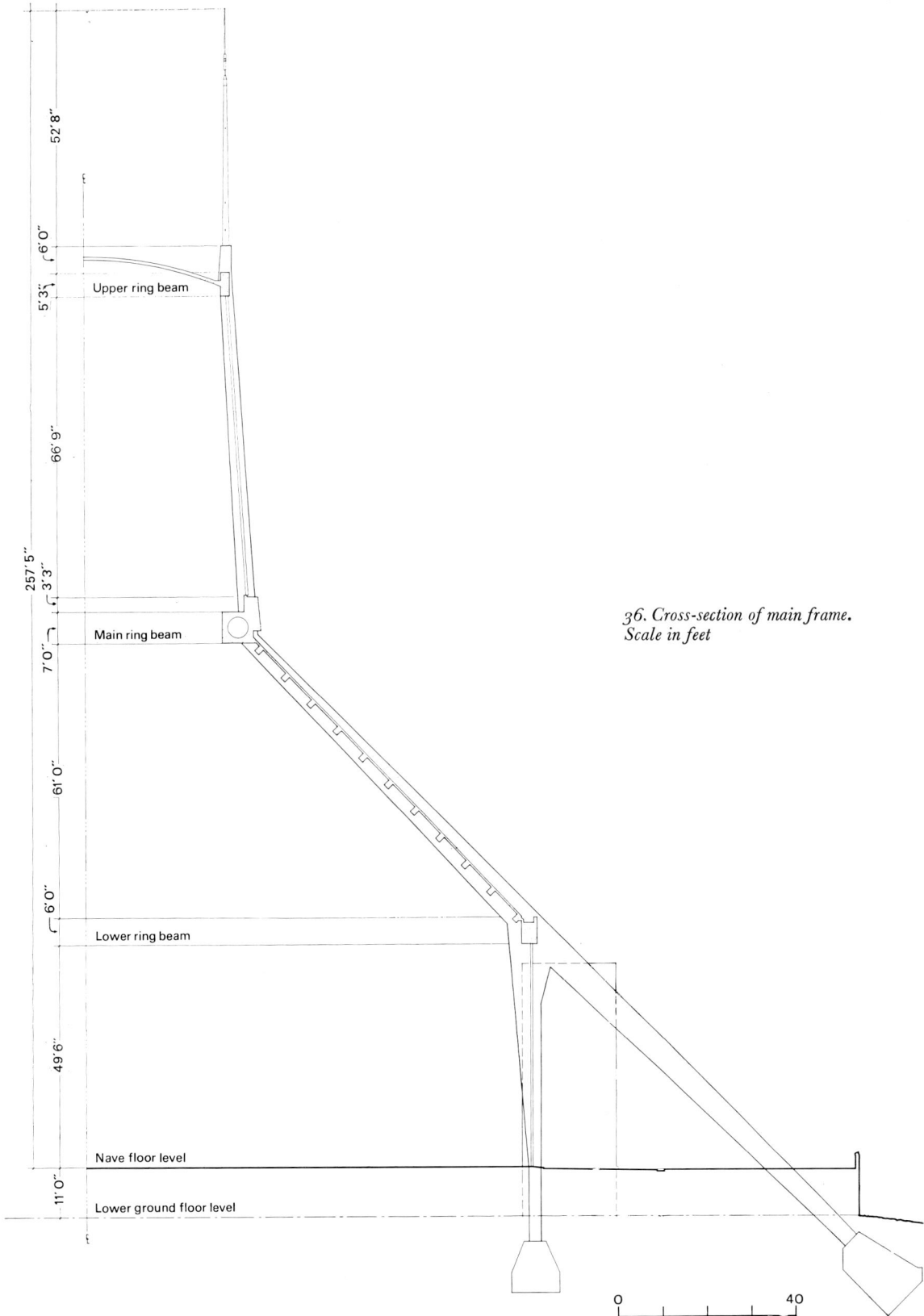

36. Cross-section of main frame.
Scale in feet

6' 0"

6' 0"

Lower ring beam

49' 6"

Nave floor level

11' 0"

Lower ground floor level

0   40

The frame has a constant width from the foundations up to the main ring beam at the base of the tower but the depth varies with the amount and direction of the forces the members carry: thus, the frame increases in depth from the ground to the lower ring beam and then diminishes to the base of the tower.

The plane of the conical roof is broken by the structural rib (the roof slabs and their aluminium surface finish are slotted into the sides of the frame); it would have been easier and cheaper just to have covered the whole structure with a roof like an umbrella, but the continuity of the frame would then have been lost to view and with it the authentic expression of the structural system. As it is, the frame is seen extending from the ground to the top of the tower (44).

The main ring beam, (34), holds the frame together at the most critical position of the change in direction of the load and also forms a base for the tower. The most effective section was a square and, to reduce the weight of the beam to a minimum, it has a hollow core formed by casting the concrete round a fibreglass tube which was later withdrawn and re-used. The outer upstanding member helps receive the tower ribs and has the appearance of a ring tying the building together where its form changes direction; in the competition design I underlined the collar-like effect by a facing of bronze plates for which, owing to the cost, were eventually substituted concrete panels faced with granite chippings.

The beam is 7 ft. square and its top could make a splendid gallery for viewing the nave but it is held in space, so there are no vertical piers like those of historic cathedrals, in which a staircase or lift could be incorporated. We could think of no method of getting people up there; devices like a lift in an open metal framework from the nave floor, or an enclosed cradle slung from the ceiling slope rather like a ski lift, proved wildly impracticable. Its only use is to provide a maintenance gallery and accommodation for electrical equipment. Access is by an external ladder on the face of one of the roof ribs; a perilous climb which will only be undertaken by the experienced or the brave.

The lower ring beam, (35), being only required to stiffen the structure, is very much less thick; the top is designed to form a hidden gutter to take the immense volume of rain water running down the face of the tower and the conical roof.

As the atmospheric conditions of Liverpool may be harmful, the external surfaces of the structural frame are clad in an off-white Swedish glass mosaic (37). Since exposed concrete surfaces are now fashionable,* there was considerable criticism of this practice of hiding it under a veneer, but it seemed to me that a light, self-cleansing surface would better express the precision of the structural form than one stained and mottled by atmospheric pollution. The structural frame was cast against a mesh of expanded metal to produce a rough texture which would adhere to the mortar on which the mosaic is bedded.

* It is said to be more truthful to expose them, but on that count one should also expose the plumbing and leave rooms unplastered.

The roof cone

The building is roofed at two levels: by a shallow saucer dome over the tower and by a section of a cone between the base of the tower and the top of the nave walls.

The conical roof is an integral part of the main structure. The sixteen frames support prefabricated concrete beams or purlins spanning between them and the purlins in turn carry prefabricated concrete infilling panels, in which are incorporated both the insulation and roof finish. The sectional diagram, (38), shows a precast rectangular purlin on which are bedded down the precast slabs.

I decided on an aluminium roof finish because, apart from the advantages of light weight and reasonable cost, I knew from the experience of Hinkley Point nuclear power station that it would weather to a soft powder-grey colour which would be within my colour range of white to dark grey. The problems of fixing the sheeting and providing insulation were exceptionally difficult ones for, apart from allowing for contraction

57

and expansion caused by shrinkage and changes in temperature, the roof had to withstand considerable suction from the wind, (40 lb. per sq. ft.).

The system devised was a composite sandwich in which aluminium sheeting is stuck down to panels of concrete by an insulating layer of foamed polyurethane. The panels were about 12 ft. by 8 ft. by 5 in. thick and were manufactured in a special shop on the site, under controlled temperature conditions.

There was a visual loss in this 'sophisticated' roofing system: the traditional jointing for sheet metal is closely-spaced parallel rolls or ridges stretching in unbroken lines from the eaves to the ridge; here the joint is flat and undecisive and there is none of the lineal pattern and texture which characterises so many cathedral roofs.

Aluminium is subject to corrosive action from a polluted atmosphere, which it resists by developing a patina or film of oxide. The atmospheric hazards of Liverpool were reduced by an ingenious idea of the consulting engineer, which amounted to running round the top of the cone a perforated water pipe, which can be turned on at intervals to wash down the aluminium.

The tower structure

The objective in the design of the tower was a homogeneous concrete and glass structure, extending out of the cone effortlessly and without rhetoric. The shape is tapered (12 ft. in a height of 82 ft.) and it is formed from the main structural frame with an infilling of coloured glass held together by epoxy resin and concrete ribs.

The sixteen ribs are held at the bottom by the main ring beam and at the top by the upper ring beam, with which is integrated the saucer dome. Unlike those below, the ribs diminish in breadth as well as width to reflect the taper of the tower and at the top their inclination is adjusted to the vertical to take the pinnacles – the pinnacles readjust the taper of the tower

38. Below: conical roof –the junction of the roof slab and the beam or purlin

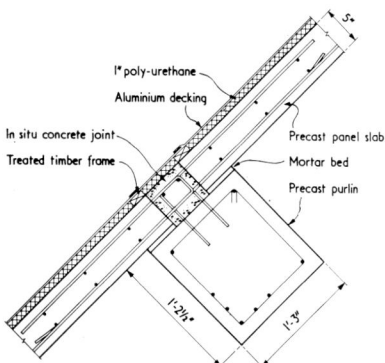

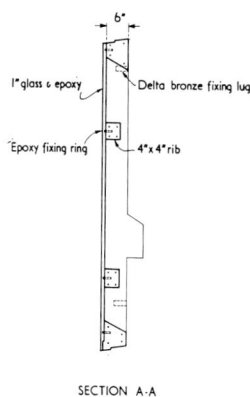

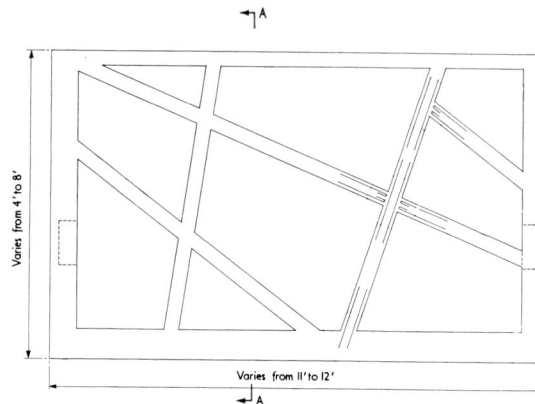

SECTION A·A

39. Below: typical pre-cast concrete glazir panel in the tower

58

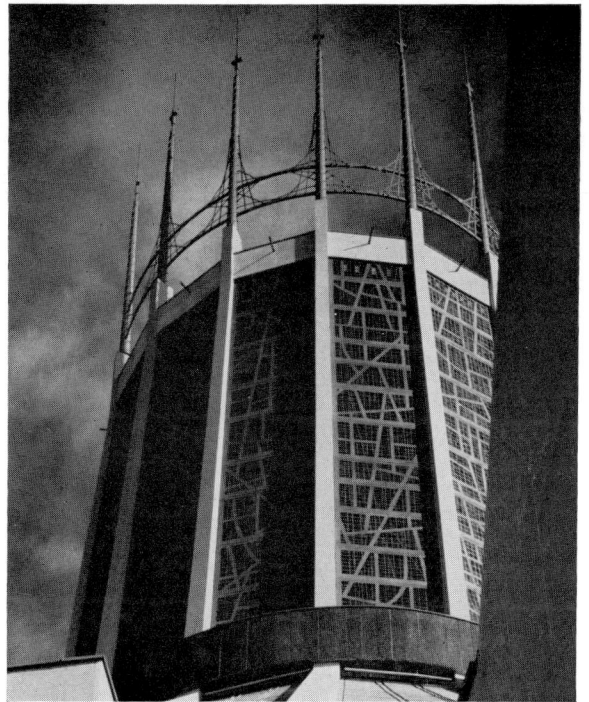

40, 41. Tracery in tower windows. Left, the original conception; right, as built

to the cylindrical form of the nave. I had originally imagined the tower as being filled with a tracery of flowing concrete ribs which would merge with the verticals to become a continuous form (40) but this proved impracticable and the design that finally emerged has an infilling of rectangular panels with straight secondary ribs (41).

Since the tower is a spatial extension of the sanctuary it will be more appropriate to consider the detail design and construction of the glass and concrete in a later chapter on the interior design.* In broad terms, the conception by John Piper and Patrick Reyntiens is of three blazes of light extending into the colour progression of the spectrum. The design ignores the structural frame altogether, the three areas of light being superimposed over the vertical ribs roughly equi-distant apart. Each of the sixteen spaces between the vertical ribs is filled with a series of rectangular glass and concrete panels about 12 ft. wide with variation in the height between 8 ft. and 4 ft., so that the horizontals do not line up together to form rings round the tower. I was concerned that the panels would give an unfortunate ladder-like effect but this is counteracted in the design by the secondary diagonal ribs extending from one frame to another.

Each panel (39, 50) was precast as a complete unit. The secondary ribs and glass areas were cemented together with epoxy resin and concrete lugs were cast on the side for fixing to corresponding lugs on the main frame. The panels were manufactured by Patrick Reyntiens' workshop, transported to Liverpool and slung into place by the tower crane.

* See page 68.

The tower is subject to considerable wind pressure and, as the precast panels are only slotted into the main vertical rib, the structure had to be braced. The problem was, of course, to prevent the bracing from confusing the appearance of the tower. The consulting engineer invented an ingenious system of trusses which occur in four opposite bays. The trusses consist of stainless steel diagonal ties in opposite directions, (two 2″ diameter rods in one direction cross one 3″ diameter rod in the other), which are held together at the top and bottom by horizontal concrete ties which occur between the joints of the precast panels. The horizontals cannot be seen and so strong is the glass design that the rods are hardly noticed.

The whole of the external face of the panels was coated with an impermeable skin of epoxy resin and, to counteract the action of ultra-violet light, slate dust was sprinkled over the resin. In certain lights, instead of a tracery of ribs, the slate dust turns the infilling panels into dark grey areas isolating the vertical frame, an unexpected effect which I regret.

The pinnacles

The pinnacle structure arose, as I have said,* from the desire to dissolve the geometric form of the tower into the hazy atmosphere of Liverpool (an environmental determinant). The pinnacles themselves, 52 ft. 8 in. high, are surmounted by spikes carrying box section crosses and the cross bracing in steel traces out a symbolic crown. The whole structure is finished a dull grey.

It was some three years before the design reached finality. I found it difficult to judge what the size and proportion of the members should be (even with the help of a full-size model held aloft by the tower crane) and the engineer was faced with complicated structural problems arising from the exposed and windy conditions. Like so many of the cathedral problems, the resultant form was evolved by combined effort.

The diagram (43) shows the idea: a composite structure of epoxy resin and concrete pinnacles braced by steel tracery, with box section steel crosses. The pinnacles themselves (one is shown being hoisted into position in the picture right (42)), consist of $\frac{1}{4}$ in. thick fibreglass and epoxy resin tubes into which the concrete was poured. The concrete was stiffened by high tensile steel reinforcement on the perimeter and by strands of steel wire passed through a hole down the centre, which were stressed down on to the main ribs of the tower. As the pinnacles might vibrate at right angles to the direction of the wind (just as a stick drawn through water vibrates), three 1 in. square p.v.c. helices are run round each pinnacle, to prevent them oscillating – I am uncertain whether or not I like the barley sugar effect.

42. A pinnacle is hoisted into place

43. Structure of pinnacles : scales in feet

stainless steel capping

$2\frac{1}{2}$ in. diameter m.s. finial plastic coated

steel cross plastic coated

4 in. diameter m.s. tube plastic coated

steel boss and hood plastic coated

upper pre-cast unit, 9 in. diameter at top
steel cleat for fixing tracery between pinnacles

in-situ junction of upper and lower pre-cast units

lower precast unit

lower precast unit 1 ft. 6 in. diameter at base

precast base block with in-situ core

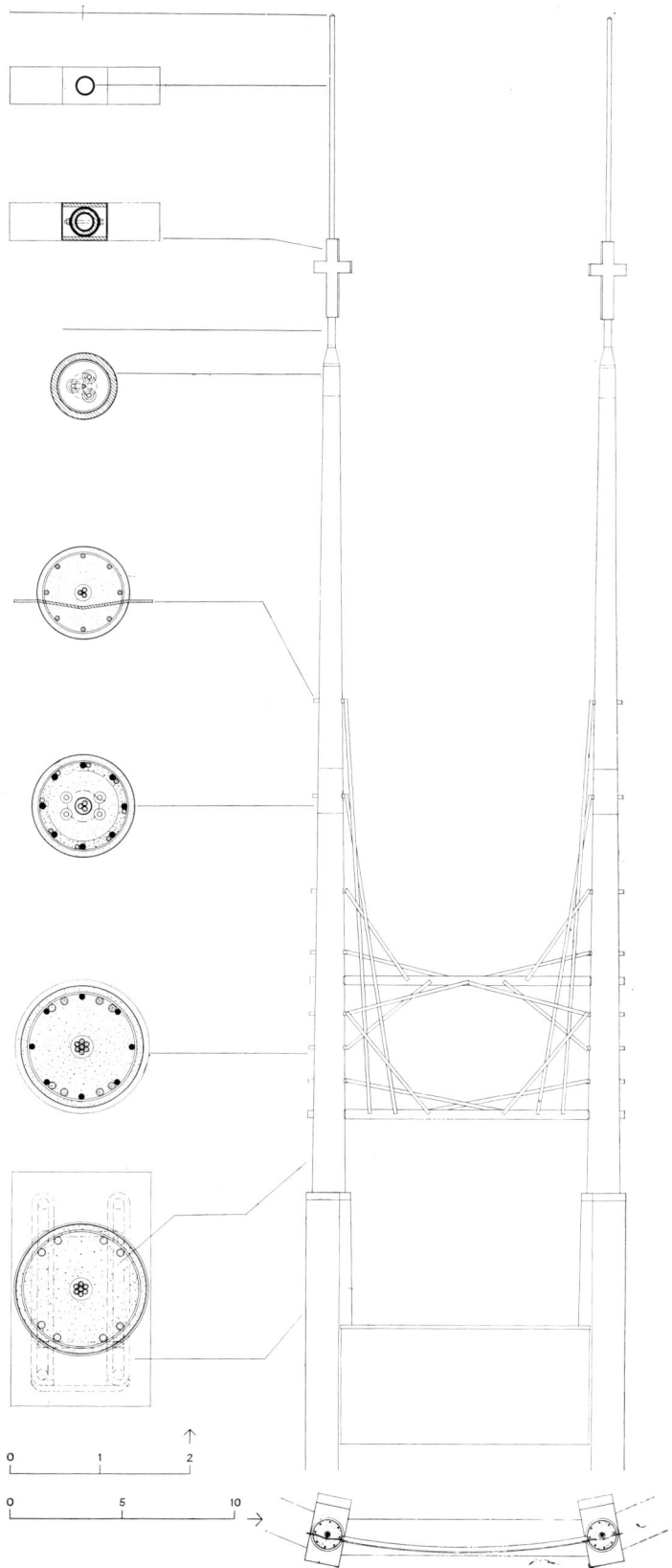

0   1   2

0   5   10

The independent load-bearing structures

The small chapels, stair towers and baptistery were originally designed as reinforced concrete structures carried on the podium itself. Through the introduction of an external veneer of Portland stone and after a detailed cost study, it was decided to build them as brick structures, independent of the podium. The walls are normally $13\frac{1}{2}$ in. brick but, where large openings are made, reinforced concrete construction was used. The two larger structures, the main porch and the Chapel of the Blessed Sacrament, remained as reinforced concrete structures and the east and west porches are framed in that material. The Portland stone, with which all these buildings are faced, is Shelley Whitbed, 3 in. thick, fixed by copper cramps.

The podium which is, again, independent of the main stucture, consists of a concrete slab carried on reinforced concrete columns, or brick walls. The external brick walls are faced with precast concrete slabs which have a surface of blue-grey Anglesey granite, providing a robust dark and textured base for the cathedral (44). The granite slabs are taken up to form a parapet round the podium and are backed with concrete block instead of brick – cost precluded granite being used for the inside face. The approach ramp is of similar construction to the podium walls.

I had originally intended to use York stone for all the pavings on the site, as this is a traditional material in Liverpool. Although I had saved considerable areas of old stone paving from the site, there was nothing like enough to pave the podium. As new York stone is costly, I considered alternative materials and remembered having seen huge tips of old slate in Wales. To my disappointment we found it impracticable to extract it for re-use but we did find quarries in production where considerable waste could be had relatively cheaply. The slate I used was a river Welsh slate from Caernarvon, of dark blue-black colour. It was laid in random pieces with irregular cement joints and, so that it would be in character with the geometry of the building, was sub-divided into 9 ft. 0 in. square panels by narrow strips of precast concrete. The dark colour and irregular texture give the appearance of a solid platform for the building and a contrast to the Portland stone of the walls (37).

In contrast to the rectangular plane of the podium, York stone is used for the staircases and ramps and the old stone was re-used for paved forecourts at ground level.

The difficult problem of draining rain water from the podium was solved by encircling the cathedral with a 12 in. wide drainage channel with 12 in. square gratings which lock into metal frames (47). As the rectangular pattern of the slate pavings is very bold, I regarded the area between this drainage grating and the walls of the chapels as being a transitional one. It is finished in concrete which has been brushed to give a texture and is sub-divided by strips of Welsh slate. The same slate is used as a skirting to the Portland stone of the chapels.

Apart from the pavings, the only other work required to complete the Lutyens crypt was on the north frontage where we built an escape staircase and roofed the two staircase towers on each corner.

44. Facing page: the dark and textured walls of the podium form a base for the cathedral

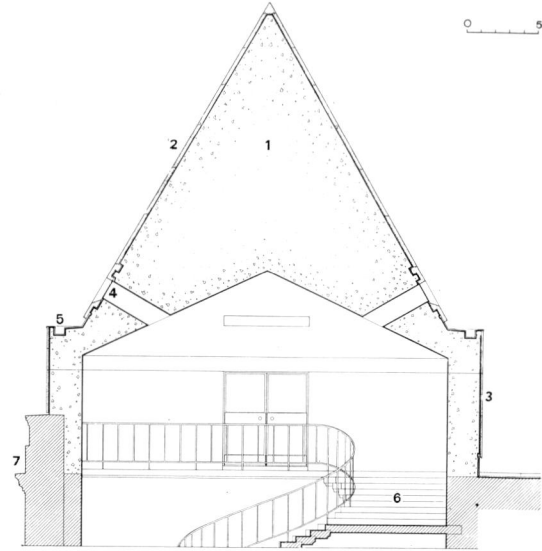

45, 46. The pyramidal
roof designed to stabilise
Lutyens stair turrets.
Scale in feet

Key:
1. Mass concrete pyramid
2. Portland stone
3. Granite
4. Roof light
5. Concealed asphalt-lined
   gutter
6. Existing granite cantilevered stair
7. Existing crypt wall

The escape stair is a simple reinforced concrete structure but the roofing of the existing staircase was a much more intriguing problem. These stairs are cantilevered out from the walls to leave a large circular well. The weight of the building was to have held the cantilever down but, as it was never completed, the outside edges of the stairs were supported by scaffolding. I therefore placed over the stairs a large block of solid concrete, the weight of which held the walls down and enabled the scaffolding to be removed. As can be seen in the diagram (46), the block is a pyramid with slots to admit light and it is faced on the outside with Portland stone.

45, 46. The pyramidal roof designed to stabilise Lutyens stair turrets. Scale in feet

Key:
1. Mass concrete pyramid
2. Portland stone
3. Granite
4. Roof light
5. Concealed asphalt-lined gutter
6. Existing granite cantilevered stair
7. Existing crypt wall

47. The podium paving, with the drainage channel which encircles the cathedral walls

64

5. THE NAVE

Unlike the traditional Gothic cathedral, in which the interior space is sub-divided into nave, crossing, transepts, choir and sanctuary, Liverpool is one continuous space embracing the nave, sanctuary and lesser elements like the choir. This one space expands outwards from the sanctuary and builds up in height through the conical roof, to reach its highest point in the tapering cylinder of the tower. The tower, as I have said, is not an arbitrary architectural form, it is an extension of the space over the high altar and it combines with the conical roof to form a vast canopy over priests and congregation alike.

The three elements that contain the space, the drum, cone and tapering cylinder, are unified by the sixteen reinforced concrete trusses which stretch upwards from the floor to the top of the tower: the unity of the space is expressed by the unity of structure.

The concrete of the frame is left without any surface finish (there was no problem of atmospheric pollution inside the building), and the texture is smooth and precise to give maximum expression to the structural form.

Since very large areas of coloured glass were to be used for the tower and the nave windows, it seemed that the other elements of the interior should be within the same muted colour range as the structural frame. The chapels are finished in a cement render of a slightly warmer grey than the concrete; the floor is grey and white marble; and timber fittings, like the seating, are in waxed oak. The exception is the conical nave ceiling, where the areas between the concrete frame are finished a very dark blue, almost black in certain lights, to subordinate that space and emphasise the tower as a brilliantly-coloured extension of the sanctuary.

From all points of view the focus of the nave is the white marble altar, the base of which is raised 2 ft. 0 in. above the floor level by the stepped sanctuary and increased in scale by the circular baldacchino suspended above it. The organ forms a major visual focus on the central axis of the cathedral and below it can be seen the reredos in the Chapel of the Blessed Sacrament: a reminder of that chapel's association with the high altar.

The nave walls

The nave has no walls in the conventional sense, but is surrounded by the lesser buildings – the chapels – which are free-standing forms, placed between the sixteen columns of the structural frame, and surrounded by coloured glass. Seen head-on against the bright light, the chapels become dissociated from the main structure; seen in sharp perspective at night they merge with it, to become massive walls. There is also considerable diversity in the spatial relationships between the chapels and the nave space (48) – some, like the Lady Chapel, are open to the cathedral and its

65

space extends into them (87); others have only a small entrance door and blend with the surrounding surface to form a wall.

The structural frame tapers in depth from the floor upwards towards the cone and, when seen at an angle, cuts across the top of the vertical lines of the chapels. In fact, the only constant external wall in the building is that formed by the narrow, vertical windows which separate the frame from the small buildings. The width of these windows was critical for, had they been too narrow, the tapering frame would have become confused with the walls of the independent buildings and, if too wide, they would have completely dissociated the frame from the independent buildings.

This complexity of forms interacting on each other causes interesting perspective effects which are complicated by the circular plan form. I found them almost impossible to draw and they can only be properly judged by visiting the cathedral.

The nave lighting

A major aesthetic decision in the design of a church is the determining of how much natural light is to be allowed in the interior and, with this, the quality of the light. A church is not a classroom nor a workshop, where even lighting conditions are required over the whole of a working surface; one element, the altar, must have the highest intensity because it is the focus, elsewhere only sufficient light is required for reading small print: any intensity above this norm is a matter of the desired atmosphere.

At Liverpool the sources of natural light are, as we have seen, the tower, which envelops the altar and the core of the nave, and the clerestory and vertical windows which light the perimeter areas; the ceiling is left, by comparison, as a dark canopy (48). The glass areas are more than sufficient to flood the nave with light but there was the particular problem, already mentioned, of a large volume of geometric form becoming boring, however impressive its first impact might be. Since my intention was that, after one had passed through the entrance porch, the space should slowly unfold itself, the problem was not how much light but how little and of what quality.

Church windows are normally obscure to avoid the distractions of the world outside. Only when there are particular circumstances is a view allowed – such as the great west window in Coventry, where it was the architect's desire to link the nave to the cathedral ruins and the city beyond. Plain obscure glass gives a very cold light and can transmit a most uncomfortable glare from the rays of the sun. Some churches are white-washed and flooded with hard light of immaculate austerity: but the people of Liverpool are not Cistercian monks and such an environment seemed to me to be inappropriate for the interior. There was, too, the aesthetic problem that a tower of the white light of clear glass would, by silhouetting the vertical ribs and by its own intensity, draw the eye up-wards, away from the altar.

Stained glass was the obvious answer: a material capable of controlling the quality of light and in itself of unique, surpassing beauty. Provided,

48. Facing page: nave interior, showing a glimpse of the Blessed Sacrament chapel between two stair towers, and right, an enclosed chapel

that is, that one could dismiss from one's mind the insipidity of countless memorial windows and other 'ecclesiastical art-works' and remember instead Gloucester, York or Chartres. "To soften the light with a pattern which made a story or picture, to turn it from dazzling blankness into a diaper or mosaic of transparent colour as deep, as radiant and as inexhaustible as that of precious stones – this was the ingenious device by which the workers in stained glass perfected architecture at the time of its transition from Romanesque to Gothic. So was added to cathedrals their most gorgeous ornament."*

At Liverpool the traditional technique of thin glass, put together in lead cames and held in a metal frame, seemed out of character with the conception of the tower as a unified concrete and glass structure – the traditional solid tower with windows set in it was the last thing I wanted. There was, too, the problem of money. The huge areas of glass involved (for it was obvious that the nave windows must also be of the same character), if manufactured to the slow and laborious craft techniques of lead cames, could be phenomenal in cost – comparatively cheap enamel stained glass of commonplace design is available but superb glass and superb design can cost anything between £15 to £30 a square foot.

The answer seemed to me be in the comparatively new techniques of casting small slabs of coloured glass in concrete, as homogeneous panels. This concrete and glass construction has a superficial resemblance to stained glass in that concrete members are substituted for cames: but there the resemblance ends. The solids are much winder and bolder and the colour of the glass itself is more intense.

The coloured glass

One of the most impressive aspects of the story of the Liverpool glass is that art ceased to be the exclusive and esoteric activity of a superior being, the artist. Everyone became involved in the design: the contractor, the consulting engineer, the architect, the quantity surveyor and a host of specialist technicians; the stained glass artists, on their part, became concerned with such technical problems as the properties of building materials, and industrialised building techniques.

The initial decision to use concrete and glass for the whole of the tower seemed at the time, to prevent some very formidable problems indeed. The glass was to cover some 12,500 sq. ft.; the greater part of it was to be fixed over 130 ft. above the ground, and all I knew of it was that 1 in.-thick glass in small squares could be cast in concrete panels: the Cathedral Committee knew even less.

Perhaps the problems facing us in the early days of the design can best be summarised by the following extracts from a report I made to Cardinal Heenan in 1962:

"As the material and the construction are different, the design must be different: in other words, the material should not be used as a cheap substitute for stained glass. Since no one but a very large organisation could produce

* Robert Sencourt, *The Consecration of Genius*, Hollis and Carter, 1947.

the quantities of glass we require and since no large organisation employs the artist of top rank that the cathedral demands, there are two problems: the manufacture and the design. The manufacturing process is a new one and has not been used on the scale of the cathedral before. Furthermore, it has never been used in an exposed and inaccessible position like the tower. I am convinced that there are potentialities in design and construction for drastically reducing the cost and the speed of erection. I see no reason why the manufacturing process should not be changed from a craft to an industrial technique, nor why the erection on the site should not be by the tower crane and other machines."

The design for the cathedral now entered its most critical stage. We were confronted with that difficult subject, art, and all the hazards of personal taste. Till then no one had questioned any design decisions, for they had been established by the competition: whether they were liked or not, no one could force me to change them; but now we were concerned with another art form and with the choice of an artist.

The outcome of my recommendations was that Cardinal Heenan went to the Church of Our Lady of Fatima in Harlow, to see for himself what concrete and glass construction looked like and followed it up by a visit to Coventry where, thanks to Sir Basil Spence, there are examples of the work of some of the best stained glass artists in the country. From that moment everything moved forward as if by destiny. Cardinal Heenan was impressed most of all by the baptistery windows at Coventry, designed by John Piper and made by Patrick Reyntiens; but they are conventional leaded construction and what I needed was experimental design work with glass and concrete. By good fortune Reyntiens was not only an established designer in his own right but had a skilled staff of technicians and a large, well-equipped workshop.

John Piper and Patrick Reyntiens were appointed joint designers and produced for the Cathedral Committee their first conception for the glass in the tower, in the form of a large painting showing three bursts of light, symbolising the Trinity, set against a background of the colour progression of the spectrum. The design ignored the concrete ribs altogether, to become an immense cylinder of coloured light. Here was a design that grasped the great scale of the cathedral, which solved all the problems of foreshortened views from the nave and one which, above all, recognised that the stained glass was an integral part of the total nave design.

The drawings of the tower were followed by a model of the nave glazed with coloured glass and large enough for members of the Cathedral Committee to stand inside.

Then the experimental work with the actual materials began. As we have seen*, the concrete and glass were to be cast in rectangular concrete frames held in each of the sixteen bays of the tower. There were 156 panels in all, twelve bays containing nine panels each and the remaining four bays, which brace the tower, contain twelve panels. Inasmuch as the largest panel weighs nearly two tons and each one contains about a

49. *Facing page, John Piper and Patrick Reyntiens at work in Henley Town Hall on the cartoons for the tower glass, and below : 50, one of the 156 panels completed*

51. *The tower glass, by John Piper and Patrick Reyntiens, represents the Trinity by its three brilliant areas of white (one is shown above) set against a background that follows the colour progression of the spectrum*

hundred pieces of glass, the task of manufacturing them was formidable and to help in its rationalisation a large workshop was built, equipped for casting concrete and for handling the panels by overhead transporters.

Experimental work began on methods of manufacture, and the first break-through was the use of epoxy resin to cement the pieces of glass together instead of concrete. The glass itself is in the form of 1-in. thick slabs measuring only 12 in. by 8 in. and the substitution of a thin dark line of resin for a wide, light area of concrete gave quite new opportunities and dimensions to the design.

Epoxy resin is a new material and the glass in the tower is exposed to very severe pressures from wind and rain. Accordingly, James Lowe arranged a series of tests with the National Physical Laboratory, which proved that the resin was more permanent and stronger than concrete. The experiments determined that no area of cemented glass should exceed 16 sq. ft. and so each frame is subdivided by concrete ribs of 4 in. by 4 in. cross section.

After the experimental work was over, Piper and Reyntiens painted full-size cartoons of each of the sixteen bays on rolls of drawing paper nearly seventy feet long and twelve feet wide, so that the designs could be seen in their entirety. Henley Town Hall was hired and three bays at a time were laid out on the floor (49). Each piece of glass was selected for its particular position; there was no standardisation or repetition of any kind – any hope I had of rationalising this particular process was soon disposed of by John Piper's remark that stained glass design was not to be reduced to the mere assembly of units like tiles. The consulting engineers checked that each area of glass came within the prescribed maximum and they marked the lines of reinforcement on the concrete ribs.

The manufacturing process of the panels was complicated and unique; I can but describe it in the very broadest terms. It was in two stages: first the pre-cast concrete frames with their cross ribs were made and then the coloured glass was placed in the frames, with epoxy resin.

The work began by Patrick Reyntiens, in consultation with John Piper, selecting each piece of coloured glass and marking its reference number on the cartoons – a formidable task in terms of the labour alone. Tracings were then made of the cartoons so that the steel reinforcement for the concrete frames could be fabricated.

Each frame was made on a steel table or form (the contractors made the formwork, to ensure that it was the exact size for the job), which was covered with polythene sheeting, on to which were stuck templates cut from the original tracings, representing each piece of glass. The glass areas were then masked out by 4-in. thick blocks of polystyrene – 4 in. being the thickness of the concrete rib. The concrete was then poured, the table vibrated to compact it and, after curing, all the surfaces were vacuum cleaned ready for the glass to be placed in position.

The joints between each segment of glass were reinforced by a cord of fibreglass and the gaps filled with a special resin mortar squeezed from a polythene bag with a small hole in one corner – rather like a cake icer. Resin mortar was then trowelled over the concrete ribs and along the edges

73

of the glass and dusted on the outside with slate dust which, having a rough matt grey finish, protects the resin from the sun's rays and obscures its unpleasant sheen.

The completed units (50) were then transported to Liverpool and fixed in place with the help of the tower crane.

It was not until the building was almost complete and all the natural light excluded that we could see the full splendour of the conception (51) and how inevitable it seemed as a part of the nave design.

The quality of the coloured light changes during the day; when the exterior is in bright sun the effect is breathtaking, and the design itself is in a constant state of change as one moves around the nave. On entering the cathedral the sanctuary is the focus, but the eye is then drawn upwards by the vertical lines of the baldacchino to a halo of colour; the closer one moves towards the sanctuary the more of the glass is revealed. The views are always so foreshortened that the tower remains truncated in form and never becomes dissociated from the sanctuary (52).

From the outside the glass appears dark with glows of colour where the sun penetrates the tower, but at night the floodlights inside the base of the tower illuminate the total design.

The nave glass was made by the same technique as that in the tower. I had felt from the beginning that the design must be subordinate to the tower and should be of continuous areas of blues and greys which, by encircling the nave, would hold it together as a unity. This conception, far removed from the conventional idea of stained glass windows as complete and individual works of art, was welcomed by Piper and Reyntiens, who designed the clerestory to be an encircling band of predominating blues fading to purples, mauves and broad areas of green, into which flecks of red are introduced, giving a horizontal rhythm.

The same colour range is used for the vertical windows but without the reds. The colours are in large, broad areas of a diagonal pattern, ignoring altogether the intervening structure, to circumscribe the nave with a total design.

In contrast to the encircling blues and greens, the east and west porches have their thin vertical windows glazed in red, which I find too obvious a contrast, albeit it underlines the secondary axis. The nave windows give the interior a constantly changing atmosphere depending on the light outside. In bright sun the diagonal shapes of colour are so intense that they tend to confuse the structural form and it might be that a rectangular pattern with less colour contrast would have been more successful. However, there is no doubt about the superb effect of the total design.

52. Facing page: foreshortened view of the tower, baldacchino in foreground

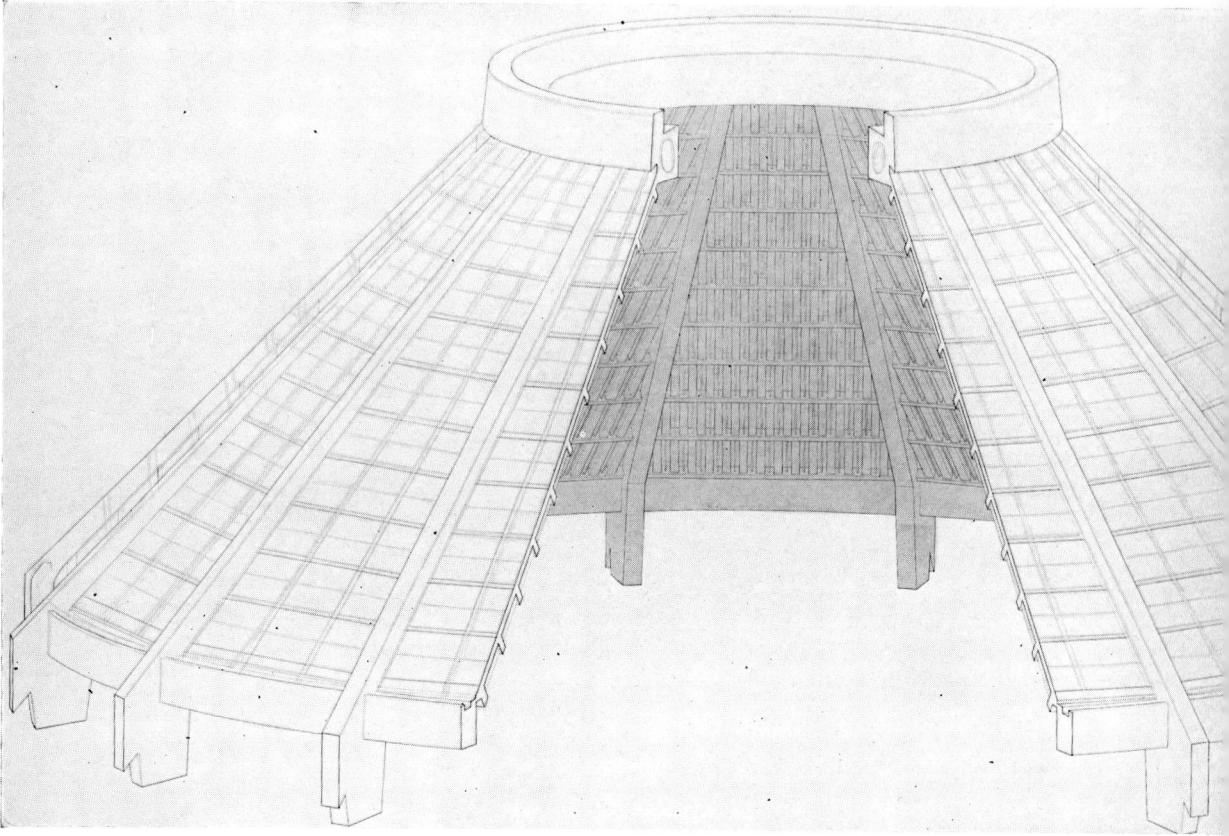

Acoustics and the roof cone

The roof cone was intended to form a dark canopy over the nave, so that attention is not diverted from the sanctuary and its crown of coloured glass in the tower. It seemed to me that it would be most effective as a dimly-lit, irregular surface with varying degrees of shadow. The underside of the concrete slab between the structural ribs forms a flat ceiling and, as I do not use decorative forms for their own sake, the ceiling would have been left flat, were it not that a broken surface was desirable as an acoustic device.

A circular building with a large void over the source of sound is by no means a good acoustic shape – Mr. Hope Bagenal, whom I consulted in the early stages, called it perverse – but, although there were major acoustic problems, they were not large in number.

On the advice of Mr. Hope Bagenal, H. R. Humphreys and Hugh Creighton were appointed acoustic consultants. The problem set and their solution, which proved entirely successful, is as follows.

In a large building all sounds are prolonged for many seconds by the echo or reverberation; succeeding sounds are masked and become incomprehensible. Speech and music are both affected by this but while musical tone, especially that of choirs and organ, is enhanced by a

76

moderately long reverberation, speech is not. The choice of the appropriate reverberation time was, therefore, of the greatest importance. (The length of the reverberation can be controlled by an appropriate choice of surface finishes for walls, floors and ceiling, and by the addition of special surfaces to reflect the sound.) A time of approximately five seconds at middle pitch with full congregation was chosen, which is similar to that found in some of the smaller mediaeval cathedrals; this ensured good musical tone and, at the same time, conditions for which a good speech reinforcement system could be designed.

It was clear that the acoustic requirements could not be answered by the use of a single material and that a complexity of surface was necessary to diffuse the sound received, as well as to absorb some of it. To answer both requirements, it was decided to form the ceiling of the nave by fixing panels between the purlins of the roof, clear of the concrete slabs, and with space between each panel. This would produce an overall coffered surface divided up by areas of deep shadow.

The cut-away diagram (53) shows the roof cone and its acoustic lining and picture (48) the finished appearance.

The panels are arranged alternately at right angles and parallel with the cone roof and each is about the size of a door. Those at right angles to the roof are 3 in. thick, of hollow construction, faced with hardboard – which was found to have the appropriate degree of resilience – fixed to timber framing. Those parallel with the roof are 6 in. thick and have on their exposed faces hardboard, lacquered dark blue. On their concealed back surfaces, which face the underside of the concrete slabs, is a 2 in. thickness of glass wool faced with perforated hardboard. In all there are 2,880 panels, each fixed at four corners to the concrete purlins.

The appearance of these panels between the receding roof beams was critical and I found it impossible to visualise the appearance from drawings or models. It so happened that at that time Cardinal Heenan had recently gone to Westminster and so I asked his permission to suspend the panels from the ceiling of the cathedral there. Whilst the experiment excited some curiosity ("It's something to do with the telly") it enabled us to judge that the form and colour would be satisfactory.

The tower was a less difficult acoustic problem, although there was a danger that sound could be trapped, causing confused reverberations to persist long after the original sound had risen up from the nave below. While the varying surfaces of the concrete and glass diffuse the sound, absorbents were also incorporated in the roof. These take the forms of asbestos sprayed on the outer edge of the dome, and glass wool on the upper surface of the suspended ceiling to absorb sound from the untreated part of the roof.

Had the nave been surrounded by a circular wall there would have been major problems through the sound being reflected back to the source but as it is, the openings in the chapels and the other buildings and the projections and recessions of the frame and the windows scatter the sound and prevent it concentrating in particular places.

In such a large building the speaking voice must inevitably be amplified, but this is not desirable for choral singing. The choir is placed near the sanctuary in order that they shall be as close as possible to the officiating priest and to the congregation, but this means they are far from walls and ceilings which would reflect and project their voices. A plywood reflecting canopy is therefore incorporated in the baldacchino to reflect the sound of the voices over the whole seating area and also to return some of it to the choir themselves so that they can hear their own singing.

The organ is behind the choir, in a gallery on the main axis of the cathedral, and the console is in the choir stalls. In this way both the instrument and the organist are in correct relationship to the singers and can speak freely into the whole body of the cathedral.

The voices of the priests officiating in the sanctuary are reinforced by a loudspeaker system incorporated in the baldacchino* and provision has been made for relaying services by loudspeakers to overflow crowds on the podium outside the building.

The acoustic treatment is designed to give optimum conditions when a full congregation is present, which will obviously coincide with the most important occasions. When only a small number of people are present, the sound absorbent effect of clothing is much reduced and thus the period of reverberation increases.

To deal with this problem, four separate positions are provided within the nave at which remote control panels can be connected and the sound amplification system corrected and adjusted while a service is in progress.

The floor design

The design of the marble floors of the cathedral posed the most interesting and difficult problems. It was desirable that the pattern should help unify the elements of the space into one total design whilst, at the same time, clearly indicating their functional relationship. On the other hand, a floor is simply a flat plane on which one walks and if the pattern is too powerful it becomes out of character and distracting.

The construction of the floors is a 6-in. thick sandwich laid over the structural floor and made up of 2 in. of foamed concrete, to insulate the nave from the car park beneath it, a layer of cement screed, in which are embedded the copper heating coils or pipes, and a final finish of $1\frac{1}{8}$-in. thick marble slabs bedded in cement.

The design of all the floors is the work of David Atkins, a young painter I met through the Royal Academy Schools. He worked part-time in the office and quickly absorbed the disciplines of building geometry, cost and the nature of building materials but it was some two years before he achieved a design that finally satisfied him – and that was after the Cathedral Committee had enthusiastically agreed an earlier solution.

The basic planning conditions that had to be met were the 3 ft. modular spacing of the seating that radiates outwards from the central sanctuary; the concentric aisles which run round the outer edge of the nave and next to the sanctuary; and the main, radial aisles leading in towards the

54. David Atkins's drawing of his nave flo design

* See page 96.

sanctuary which, being processional ways, had to be of constant width, unlike all the other lines of the pattern, which widen as they radiate out from the centre. On the face of it the problem sounds easy enough, given a knowledge of geometry, a pair of compasses and a protractor; but the task was the difficult one of solving a series of complex inter-related problems. Thus it was necessary to produce a total design: that is, a design that embraced all the elements of porches, chapels, nave and sanctuary as one, unifying element; that total design had to establish a firm, directive orientation, with the sanctuary as its climax; and the floor design had to recognise the quality and scale of the volumes above it, for the cathedral is not a flat plan but a series of spaces.

To avoid the danger referred to, of the floor pattern becoming too powerful and distracting, the marble colours are subdued and limited to white, a dark dove grey and a small area of lighter grey in the sanctuary. The finish, moreover, is honed (smoothed with carborundum grit), to avoid the patches of reflected light that occur with a more highly polished surface.

The design is shown in the artist's drawing (54) on the last page. It begins in the main entrance porch, where it hesitates, to recognise the volume above it; it quickens through the low connecting link, expands into the vast space of the nave, where it echoes the sixteen concrete frames of the trusses and then focusses on to the sanctuary where it reaches its climax.

The grey marble is used as a background to lines of white marble which radiate out from the sanctuary to the surrounding chapels. But on the aisles the lines are parallel to each other, thus establishing the main axes of the building and the processional ways.

The white lines are of constant width and so the grey areas diminish towards the centre, until they are completely taken over by the white area surrounding the sanctuary – a grey perimeter area is slowly and with deceptive simplicity dissolved into a halo of white.

The sanctuary design resolved the difficult problem of relating the rectangular predella, or stepped platform, upon which the high altar stands, to the circular plan form – a design solution we shall examine in detail later.*

The pattern is also developed from the east and west porches and relates the open spaces of the Lady Chapel and the two staircase towers (where it turns back on itself in a most ingenious manner) and moves finally into the Blessed Sacrament Chapel.

Artificial heating and lighting

The nave is heated by warming its marble floor. Over the concrete structural floor is laid a two-inch layer of lightweight foamed concrete to insulate the nave from the unheated car park beneath. Between the insulation and the marble floor over the whole nave area is another layer of cement in which are embedded copper tubes. Through these, hot water is circulated from the boiler house which was built to serve the Lutyens

* See page 90.

crypt. The very large area of marble floor, when warmed, is sufficient to heat the vast space of the nave. The nave windows are a source of cold: so fan-assisted convector radiators are placed under them and supplementary convector heaters are provided in the side chapels. As the glass in the tower is also a source of cold down-draught, radiators are provided on the ring beam at the base of the tower and on the baldacchino; these, being in remote positions, are electric.

The artificial lighting was an exceptionally difficult problem for the lighting consultant J. W. J. Leslie as, apart from providing proper standards of illumination, his scheme had to draw attention to the visual foci of the interior, without conflicting with the architectural forms. He had also to contend with an aversion I have for light fittings – they tend to clutter up an interior and they draw attention to themselves, both by their design and character as sources of illumination.

55. *Nave light fitting*

Wherever possible the sources of artificial light are concealed, so that it is treated as a service to be used when daylight fades, rather than an element of design in itself. The nave area is so large we had to suspend a pendant from each of the sixteen bays of the cone roof. I avoided the problem of 'decorative' light fittings by simply assembling three commercial 750-watt tungsten iodine lamps bracketed from a central tubular stem and screening them by a black metal casing (55).

Simple spotlight fittings are placed at the back of the nave windows, to light the outer perimeter of the nave and illuminate the glass when seen from the podium and spotlights occur in other positions where it was impossible to recess a light fitting.

The glass in the tower is illuminated at night by concealed flood lights on the main ring beam, so that the external view at night echoes the internal view during the day.

The nave seating

One of the splendours of the great European cathedrals is their uninterrupted floor space which, beautiful in itself, both unifies and contrasts with the piers and columns springing upwards from the flat horizontal plane. There is seldom more than a handful of seats and in the past there were none at all, for the faithful who crowded the nave stood or knelt; only the clergy were provided with the fine architectural setting of their stalls. Today everyone expects to be able to sit, with disastrous consequences to the appearance of interiors. Seldom beautiful in themselves, seats clutter up the nave and, when not occupied, give to the building a sense of emptiness and loneliness – Coventry was a different building before chairs obliterated the floor. It is not, moreover, only a matter of appearance for, as has been said, the rigid formality of seating "can encourage a 'spectator' attitude in the congregation, as the seated area appears to be the 'public' part of the building and the sanctuary to be the 'performing' part, which the congregation merely observes".*

* Wilfred Cantwell 'Design of Churches' in *Vatican II: the Liturgy Constitution*, ed. Flannery, Scepter Publishers Ltd., Dublin 1966.

Conditioned as we are by the comforts of Western civilisation, there is small likelihood of even the most devout tolerating a church without seating. The problem is, then, to devise a plan which relates the people both to the sanctuary and to each other as a community, and which does least visual harm to the nave. We have already discussed the advantages of a circular plan form: that it can give a grouping which focusses naturally on the sanctuary and can establish a relationship of person to person in the communal act of worship. The problems of appearance hinge on three broad factors: the relationship of the seating to the floor pattern (assuming, of course, that the floor pattern is an expression of the plan form), the ease with which seats can be removed and the design of the seating itself.

At Liverpool the plan of the nave seating is fan-shaped, spread out around three sides of the sanctuary, sub-divided into blocks by the three principal aisles on the main axes and again sub-divided by secondary aisles – to conform to the fire regulation that the centre of any seat should not be more than 14 ft. from a gangway. The concentric rows are at 3 ft. centres and coincide with the joint lines of the floor pattern.

The normal seating is for a congregation of 800, concentrated round the sanctuary, to leave broad expanses of uncluttered floor. On special occasions the seating can be increased to 2,020; in addition there are 140 seats in the galleries over the two porches and 58 in the choir enclosure. This total of 2,218 is not the absolute limit of the capacity, for seating can extend into the secondary spaces associated with the nave.

Fire regulations required that seats must be fixed together in minimum groups of four and that they must be firmly fixed to the floor. The Committee favoured benches rather than chairs because benches are more flexible: a small child can be wedged in between parents rather than occupy a complete seat. Of more importance to me was that benches gave the opportunity of joining the backs and seats together as continuous, unbroken, curved planes encircling the sanctuary; and it enabled the legs to be reduced to the minimum number.

Whilst the curved seating establishes a satisfactory relationship to the sanctuary, it sets difficult design and manufacturing problems, because each row has to be of exact yet individual length, to line up with the aisles, and the radii of the rows have to vary to conform to their distance from the nave centre (56). The manufacturing problems were further complicated by the requirement that the benches, although rigidly fixed to the floor when in use, had to be capable of being easily taken up and stacked for storage. No bench on the market met these requirements and there was little prospect of getting a satisfactory design without some original thought and experiment in the joiner's shop. Accordingly, eight prominent furniture manufacturers were given the problem and invited to submit designs. From these a design by Frank Height was chosen to be developed in conjunction with the manufacturers: prototypes were commissioned and, after modifications and adjustments, a new form for church seating was reached.

The basic material is Douglas fir, which is laminated to form separate seat and back units, accurately curved to the radii of the building (57).

56. The nave seating set out on the floor pattern

82

57. Nave seating
designed by Frank
Height, showing
laminated construction

Compared with solid timber planks, the laminated construction involves
no interruption of the pattern of the grain, and both the seat and back can
be sloped – almost impossible with conventional construction. The seat and
back are joined together and supported by simple standard leg frame units,
the rear leg being carried up to support the back of the seat. To increase
structural strength and resistance to knocks, the leg frames are made of ash,
similar in colour to the Douglas fir. The seating units formed in this way
can be easily stacked away when not required.

The position of the leg frames was determined by reference to the pattern of the marble floor. In every case, the leg frames coincide with a grey area of marble and, where appropriate, they follow the radiating lines to give the least possible interruption to the pattern.

Both the Douglas fir laminated members and the ash leg frames are left in natural colour with a waxed finish and give the visual pleasures both of a natural organic material and of precision techniques in timber construction. To me, these benches, modest as they are, are design of the highest order: they reject the present fashion for heavy 'organically-shaped' solid timber benches; and reduce everything to the simplest possible terms of functional, elegant form.

6. THE SANCTUARY

The main elements of the sanctuary (61) are a platform raised 10 in. above the floor with two steps, in the centre of which is the high altar, which is raised on a platform, or predella, of three steps, the whole being surmounted by a canopy or corona which is, again surmounted by the coloured halo of the tower. The secondary elements are the Communion rails encircling the sanctuary, a movable ambo or lectern and the Bishop's throne.

Canons' stalls, traditionally associated with the sanctuary, are not provided, as the Cathedral Committee regarded them as a relic of the days when cathedral chapters consisted of a large number of resident canons or, in some cases, monks, who sang daily the full office of the church. At Liverpool nearly all the canons are parish priests who meet in the cathedral only once a month for a token singing of office and a Capitular Mass. Instead, therefore, of monumental and immovable stalls, only movable prie-dieus and chairs are provided.

At the consecration of the cathedral the sanctuary proved to be more than adequate in size, although the Bishop's throne was placed on the nave floor on the left of the sanctuary. During the mass the priests found that they were unconsciously following definite patterns in moving about the sanctuary and afterwards the celebrant, Bishop Harris, told me that the circular form gave all kinds of potentialities for new and significant ritual.

The high altar

The focus of the cathedral is the high altar (61) placed on the centre of the sanctuary, so that mass can be said either in front or behind it. In this position it is the fulcrum or pivotal point around which the cathedral is formed – the altar covers the original point on the ground from which the design and construction of the entire cathedral was set out.

The high altar is the sacred altar of sacrifice, not merely a support for flower vases or other ornaments. An altar is a table and, although originally often made of wood, it must now be of natural stone. The conventional table form of flat top and legs can look incongruous with a very large altar, particularly in stone or marble and, no doubt for this reason, they are usually enclosed or partially enclosed structures of solid appearance.

The size required was 12 ft. long by 4 ft. wide by 3 ft. 6 in. high and, although Catholic liturgy allows almost any form (providing the corners are square and the stone top is supported by stone), it seemed to me that this was no occasion for individual expression: rather that the solution was a solid block of stone or marble. This would avoid the design problems of the assembly of different members and would give the altar the qualities

of denseness and timelessness of the living earth out of which it was hewn. White is the purest of colours and marble the finest rock and so I decided to use a block of white marble without blemish, cut to a precise geometric form and polished just sufficiently to bring out the quality of the material.

The stonemasons who were providing the marble flooring knew of these intentions (anyone could know, for they were mentioned in the report on the competition), and they took the initiative of searching Europe for a block of white marble which they ultimately and literally ran to earth near Skopje in Macedonia, Jugoslavia. It was a giant, flawless block, some fourteen feet long and weighing over twenty tons which, after being quarried, was shipped to Liverpool via Italy (where it was inspected in detail) and unloaded by a special mobile crane (58).

The size was reduced to that required for the high altar, first by machine and ultimately by hand finishing, not to the familiar shiny white surface of statuary marble but a very fine non-reflective texture, to reveal the crystalline quality of the marble. Its final weight, when placed in position, was eight tons. The marble remaining from the original block was used for the altars in the Blessed Sacrament Chapel and Lady Chapel and for the font.

The crucifix and candlesticks

A high altar is required to carry a crucifix and six candlesticks. They are ranged in a straight line along the altar with the crucifix in the centre, overtopping the candles and clearly visible to the priest and people.

It was my original intention that the crucifix, with a figure slightly larger than life size, should be suspended from the baldacchino over the altar. The idea was abandoned through cost and indecision and Elizabeth Frink was commissioned to design a bronze crucifix, some three feet high, to be carried on a base designed by Professor R. Y. Goodden, who was also asked to design the candlesticks.

Elizabeth Frink produced an elegant figure with the arms fully stretched, enabling the horizontal member of the cross to be eliminated. She described her design in a letter to me as follows. "I made it as simply as I possibly could and without the usual representation of the cross. The section through the sculpture is very thin, as I felt that something refined and elegant was required. I also made the figure very fluid in movement and form all the way through, so as to make a silhouette rather than a solid sculptural shape, my main problem being to produce something that would show up well in the powerful design and space of the interior."

I had some qualms that the break from the convention of a Christ in the form of a Y, pinioned by nails to the arms of a cross, would be unacceptable to the Cathedral Committee but they welcomed the design: in particular, the suggestion of blessing given by the outstretched arms.

The design (59) was modelled in plaster and then cast in bronze by Fiorini & Carney. The finish is a patina of light gold to catch the light, and it is lacquered against tarnishing.

A feature of so many large sanctuaries is the tall candlesticks and the candles thrusting upwards from the horizontal plane of the altar. Clearly such an arrangement is undesirable when the priest is behind the altar as they would fence him in from the congregation.

It was decided that the candlesticks and base for the crucifix should be in silver and the unusual problem set Professor Goodden was to produce a design which offered the least possible obstruction of the priest whilst at he same time being significant in the large scale setting of the sanctuary.

His solution (60) was based on weighty geometric forms which have the character of a strong silver plinth on which a candle stands, rather than a candlestick. The candles themselves are $2\frac{1}{2}$ in. in diameter and 9 in. high and are held on prickets (spikes) only 3 in. above the surface of the altar. Short shafts beneath the prickets are set in square bases with sloping sides (9 in. by 9 in. and 2 in. deep), into the top surface of which are recessed shallow circular grease cups. The grease cups and pricket shaft are detachable: they can be dipped into hot water to float off the grease.

In consultation with Elizabeth Frink the same design of base was adapted for the crucifix by replacing the grease cup and pricket with a slender tube of silver, 3 ft. 6 in. in length and $\frac{5}{8}$ in. in diameter, through which runs a $\frac{1}{2}$ in. thick stainless steel rod threaded at the top to screw into the bronze crucifix, which is thus held clear above the head of the officiating priest.

The surfaces of silver have been finely scratch-brushed after polishing, to give a finish which will change as little as possible with use. The silversmiths were Wakely and Wheeler of London.

This most original solution is exactly right for the situation. The robust

59. The crucifix by
Elizabeth Frink

60. Below: the high
altar candlesticks by
Professor R. Y. Goodden

bases form a strong rhythm across the top of the altar and when seen obliquely their lines merge into a larger composition.

The sanctuary floor

David Atkins' conception of the marble floor pattern of the cathedral was, as we have seen, to extend it over all the elements as one unified composition. The sanctuary floor is not an intricate, highly ornamental design of rare and precious materials set like a jewel in the nave floor. It is of the same grey and white marble as the nave and reflects the total design; but the scale is reduced towards the altar, just as the basic elements are themselves reduced.

The design problem was a difficult one because the circular plan form has a rectangle imposed on it (the altar platform), and a rectangular form abstracted from its centre (the altar itself). The building form dictated a symmetrical pattern and the qualities of the marble floor slabs are at their most characteristic when cut into geometric shapes. The problem was, then, to design an overall pattern of contrasting grey and white forms, over which is superimposed the lineal pattern of the joints, which is reduced in scale and increased in complexity from the outer circle to the inner rectangle.

The final design (56), is of the greatest subtlety. The pattern echoes the basic form of the building and the sixteen main frames of the structure but avoids placing emphasis on any particular point of the circumference of the sanctuary.

The difficult problem was that of reconciling the rectangular altar to the circular sanctuary and, in particular, to establish a satisfactory articulation at the four corners of the raised predella (the step on which the altar stands). A solution was found by the introduction of a white border around the base of the predella, to which three linear elements are related at each corner. In this way a continuity of design is established over the whole area.

The scale of the pattern is reduced on the predella and a lighter dove grey marble was used. The varying white edge contains four white bars centrally placed on each side and which point to the centre of the white altar, which is itself the climax of the floor design.

The baldacchino

Liturgical tradition has it that no altar is complete without being surmounted by a canopy or baldacchino. This may be cantilevered out from the wall, supported on columns or suspended by chains from the roof. Magnificent as Bernini's columnar structure is at St. Peter's, it is obvious that this form in Liverpool's open plan would cause serious physical and visual obstruction to the altar and so the form adopted was a baldacchino suspended from the ring beam at the bottom of the tower.

61. *The Gospel is read during the Mass of consecration, Whitsunday, May 14, 1967. At the bottom left, Cardinal Heenan, the Papal Legate, occupies the throne. This photograph shows the cathedral abnormally full. Under normal conditions the congregation do not sit behind, the altar as diagram (6) shows*

The baldacchino is of the same diameter as the sanctuary and is suspended some thirty feet above it, so that the two elements are drawn together as one composition, in scale with the nave. But it is also an important part of the interior as a whole: the form reflects the sixteen structural frames of the building, relating the sanctuary to the nave and roof above, and acts as a transitional form between the sanctuary and the tower which illuminates it.

The design is an aluminium space frame, (a space frame is a structure like a grid, but in three dimensions instead of two), which takes the form of sixteen anodised aluminium triangular trusses which both radiate out from the centre of the building and diminish in height towards the centre where they stop short to leave a void over the altar. Diagonal bracing between the trusses, of aluminium members and strip wire, interweaves to form a light tracery.

Anodised aluminium tubes, fixed vertically from the bracing, give an upward direction to the design and were intended to be a means of providing artificial light. A light bulb was sunk into the bottom of each tube but the effect was disastrous for, in spite of the bulbs being recessed, the lights formed a starlike pattern, reminiscent of the canopy over a merry-go-round. I scrapped the outer bulbs, increased the intensity of those in the inner ring and screened them from view. Spotlights fixed to the suspended nave fittings counteract the downward direction of the baldacchino lighting and illuminate the aluminium members.

The baldacchino is also a means of taking care of such functional devices as an acoustic sounding board and artificial heating and lighting. The acoustic sounding board consists of oak-veneered plywood coffers held between the upper members of the space frame and are inclined upwards to reflect the sound into the nave.

All speech comes from somewhere within the sanctuary and so the baldacchino was a perfect position for the loudspeakers: the natural voice and the sound from the speakers always come from approximately the same direction and so the congregation is unaware of amplification. The loudspeakers, in the form of columns ten feet long ('line source loud-speakers') are ranged round the outer area of the space frame and inclined at an angle between the diagonal members to throw the sound over the whole of the seating area. The sound produced is directional, in the form of a flat fan-shaped beam, projected down on to the congregation, which ensures that little sound goes up into the tower, where it would reverberate.

To counteract cold downdraughts from the tower, sixteen electric heating panels are fixed to the baldacchino close to the centre opening, placing a blanket of warm air over the officiating priests.

The baldacchino is hung from the ring beam by sixteen cables $\frac{3}{8}$ in. thick, of galvanised steel wire, from the bottom of which thirty-two short cables collect up the load from the baldacchino itself (62). This is, on the face of it, simple enough, were it not for the problem of getting the electric cables across from the baldacchino to the main structure. There are about twenty-five cables which would be unsightly if just clipped to the suspen-sion wires. The solution devised by the manufacturers, the consulting

62. Top anchorage and lower end of cable supporting baldacchino

Key: 1. Upper cable anchorage
2. Access for electric cables and height adjustment
3. Main ring beam
4. 3 in. diameter plastic sleeve
5. Bronze cover plate
6. ⅜ in. diameter suspension cable
7. 2 in. black polythene tube
8. Stainless steel braiding
9. Braiding wrapped with stainless steel wire
10. Lower cable anchorage
11. Steel shackles
12. Steel pulleys
13. Steel secondary cables

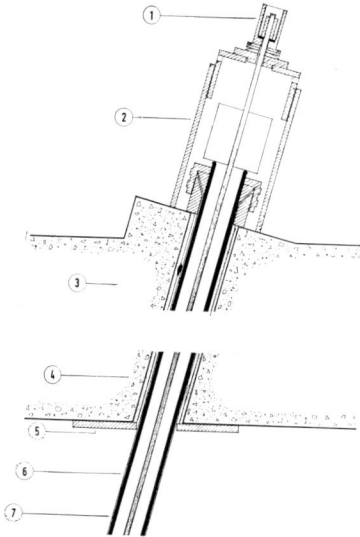

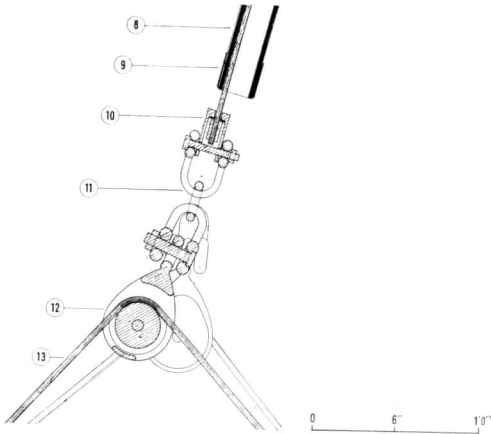

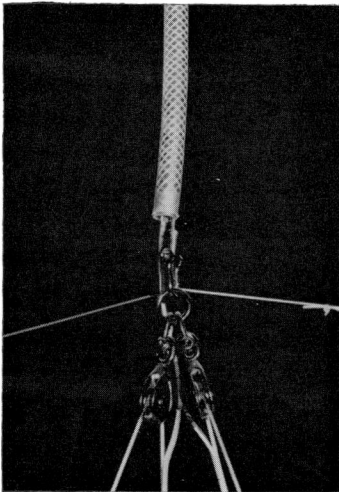

63. The braided casing
of the cable

engineer and ourselves is shown in the drawing opposite (62). The suspension wires and the electric cables are threaded through a black polythene tube of 2 in. diameter. As sixteen black tubes could look very unpleasant stretching across the cathedral space and as, being in short lengths, they had to be stiffened, there is an outer casing of braided stainless steel wire. For those interested in numbers it may be said that 160 wires of 1/20,000 in. diameter and a total length of four miles are woven together to make each casing – the braiding reflects a pleasant sheen of light.

The Bishop's throne

The Bishop's throne, or cathedra, has from early times been of elaborate design to symbolise the power and authority of the Bishop.

The relationship of the throne to the sanctuary is a subject of some controversy now that discussion of the liturgy is in fashion. At first it was placed in a semi-circular space behind the altar with seats for the higher clergy ranged on each side; it was later moved to the Gospel (left) side of the altar but there is now no generally accepted position.

The Cathedral Committee took the attitude from the outset that, since there was no instruction and since there was little experience of the use of a circular sanctuary, the throne should be portable. Although they have been criticised for indecision, they were undoubtedly right, for they are now able to experiment in establishing the most satisfactory relationship and, furthermore, there is the advantage that the throne can be moved away when the Bishop is absent.

At the consecration, the throne was placed on the nave floor on the left of the sanctuary and some seventy feet away from the altar. It was occupied by the Papal Legate, Cardinal Heenan (61, 64), who could be clearly seen in a setting worthy of his office: the arrangement also had the advantage that the pageantry was spectacularly extended into the body of the cathedral.

The elements of the design are a raised dais, on which stands a throne with canopy, on either side of which are stools for the assistant priests.

Since the throne stands in a space, it was desirable that it should offer the least possible obstruction to view and as, when not in use, it is moved into the elliptical space of a staircase tower, weight was an important consideration.

The design problem was given to Professor R. D. Russell and his drawing (66) and the picture (65) illustrate his solution. The whole design of three stools and platform is treated as a unified and simple setting for the splendidly-robed Archbishop (64).

The construction is of English oak, which is handled in a direct and robust manner stressing the essential qualities of the material. The difficult problem of supporting the canopy is solved by extending the chair legs upwards as supports, which give scale to the throne with minimum visual obstruction.

The loose cushions of the throne have interchangeable covers in each of the four seasonal colours – red, purple, green and white. A loose panel

in the canopy repeats the colour of the cushions. The carpet of the platform is handwoven in wool and horsehair and incorporates the four liturgical colours. It was designed and made by Peter Collingwood.

To make its transfer easy and rapid, the platform is provided with a hydraulic jacking system which brings four castors into operation.

64. At the consecration ceremony, Cardinal Heenan occupied the bishop's throne

65. The bishop's throne

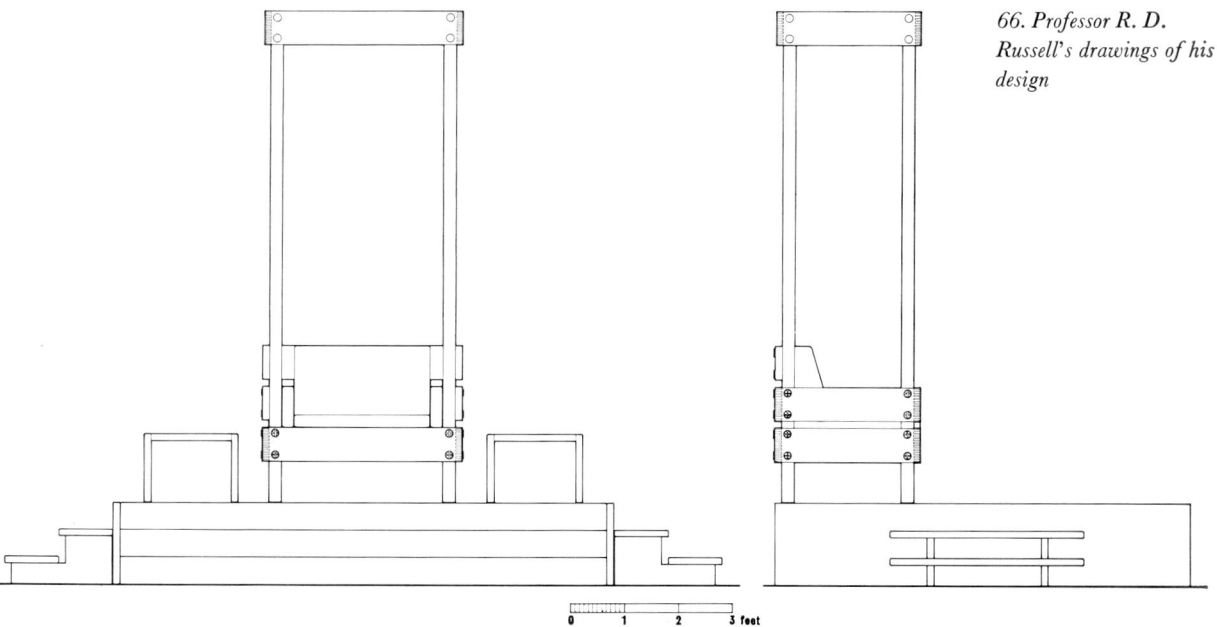

66. Professor R. D. Russell's drawings of his design

0   1   2   3 feet

7. THE ORGAN AND CHOIR

Although the design of a cathedral is directed towards making the sanctuary the focus, there are often other elements which may well exercise their own authority in the composition. Of these the organ is of considerable value because of its unique form, to say nothing of its size.

The simple functional requirements for the organ's position is that it should be an open and elevated one where the instrument can speak freely to the congregation. It may also be reasonably close to the choir so that music reaches the congregation from the same direction, in order to avoid unnecessary acoustic problems being set up. A prominent position is also desirable aesthetically for, apart from being a splendid object in itself, it symbolises the profound contribution church music has made to art.

There are great difficulties in meeting these requirements with the long, mediaeval plan. The splendid silhouettes of organs, like Lincoln and York, where they are placed above the choir screen, are no longer relevant now that the clergy have come into the body of the church. When the organ is placed over the reredos, as at Ely, it may be too prominent and conflict with the altar: but when, on the other hand, it is on one side of the choir, its full beauty is lost to distant views. Remote control by electricity now enables the organ to be in two symmetrical units on either side of the choir, as at Coventry, but it loses much of its importance. Where the organ can and does so often look magnificent is over the west entrance doors where it is the focus of the nave vista in the opposite direction to the sanctuary. But here the congregation separates the two sources of music: choir and organ, which in a long nave become remote from each other.

All these problems dissolve with a centralised plan like Liverpool because it is possible to place the organ on the central axis of the cathedral opposite the entrance. It can be expressed as one single composition, adding considerably to the splendour of the nave, and as the organ is well behind the sanctuary, there is no fear of visual conflict. With the choir placed between the sanctuary and the organ all sound comes from the same direction and the open position of the organ enables it to speak freely into the full body of the nave.

The organ

As every cathedral organ is specially built, the design requires very specialised knowledge and the closest collaboration between the musical consultant and the organ builders; all that the architect is concerned with is the appearance of the pipes and console and their relationship to the other elements – that, of course, apart from providing the necessary housing.

The Liverpool organ was built by J. W. Walker & Sons who have been

67. *The organ seen from the ramped processional approach to the nave*

making organs since 1828 and the specification was drawn up in consultation with the Revd. R. R. Wright osb, who, by good fortune, was a member of the Cathedral Building Committee.

Although the splendid instrument they designed is called an organ, it is in fact a complex of six, with a total of 4,566 pipes. As a piece of mechanism the specification sounds rather like that for a computer: 1,790 electro-magnets; 4,627 individual circuits and contacts; and 25 miles of wiring.

My problem was comparatively simple but none the less important: to give the design the maximum visual significance, both on its own account and as a focus of the nave. Although, in the nineteenth century, design deteriorated into providing a mere 'frontage' of false pipes and decorative effects like stencilled patterns, the organs at the Royal Festival Hall and at Coventry Cathedral showed that, if the grouping of the pipes is taken as the basis for the design, the maximum expression of the organ as a musical instrument can be obtained.

The pipes had to be selected and arranged to fit within the organ gallery space of 22 ft. wide and 40 ft. high. Almost half of the pipes, those of the swell and solo organs, are enclosed in timber chambers, out of sight at the back of the gallery. From the balance the largest and most interesting pipes were selected to stand in the front ranks, the remaining being grouped behind to become less and less visible the further back they are in the gallery. The design is not, therefore, a flat frontage of pipes but a plastic three-dimensional grouping which diminishes in perspective, and is at its most effective when seen at an acute angle (67).

There are four distinct visual types: cylindrical and tapering pipes of zinc, square pipes of timber and comparatively short, flared pipes of zinc with copper mouths. The pipes are grouped together in registers to emphasise their characteristic forms and so that they are convenient for tuning – a process which was a continuous operation occupying some months after the organ was installed.

The pattern finally devised, after long sessions with coloured chalks, is shown in the photograph (68). The organ's position on the main axis of the cathedral demanded a symmetrical composition but, as no two pipes are alike, the aim was to obtain a balance about the centre line rather than a mirror symmetry.

The largest pipes of all are placed in the centre with the very smallest at their feet, to emphasize as much as possible the great size of the organ. The square wood pipes, having no light-reflecting qualities, are ranged on each side of the gallery as a solid base, with overlapping zinc pipes to link them to the large central ones. The remaining tubular pipes are in four groups raised in the air on cantilevered brackets, in such a way that there is a maximum area of pipes exposed to view. I found that the flared pipes would not fit happily into vertical groupings and hit on the idea of projecting them out at right angles to the vertical clusters so that they give the splendid effect of trumpets blaring across the nave.

68. The organ in its gallery above the entrance to the Blessed Sacrament Chapel

The choir enclosure

The choir enclosure, on the main axis of the cathedral between the sanctuary and the entrance to the chapel of the Blessed Sacrament, is wedge-shaped in plan. The area is defined by a simple pine veneered screen four feet high which follows the lines set by the pattern of the marble floor.

Four crescents of seats facing the sanctuary are set on a wooden floor stepped so that the standing choir may easily see the conductor who is between them and the sanctuary. A wooden floor was used to give resonance to the singing; it acts as a sounding board. The seating provides for a total number of 50 choristers, of whom about 30 are boys, with 20 men. The enclosing screens and stepped floor are removable so that additional seating or new seating arrangements can be adopted for special occasions.

One of the major drawbacks of the plan is the organ console, which must be in a fixed position because of the organ pedal rods controlling swell and solo expressions. These are taken through a hole in the floor, along the car park ceiling and up a vertical duct beside the chapel entrance, to the organ chamber. All other connections between console and organ chamber are by large numbers of electrical cables.

There will always be a conductor for the choir and as it is essential that he is seen by the organist, the console is placed so that the organist has his back to the sanctuary but is within easy sight of the conductor who stands to his right. To enable the organist to follow the action of the mass, which takes place behind him, a small 'driving' mirror is fixed to the console light fitting set over the keyboard.

The organist is screened from public view by an etched perspex screen on top of the choir enclosure.

The choristers sit in pairs on short bench seats which were adapted in design from the standard nave seat. They stand to sing, and so it was necessary to have large reading desks mounted on the backs of the benches. These desks are made of grey anodised aluminium and are adjustable in height to allow for rearrangement of the choir (more boys or the boys in a different position). The conductor has a special movable wooden dais and bench with music stand and book store.

8. THE PORCH AND BELL TOWER

The main entrance porch and bell tower is a free-standing building approached from the southern forecourt by ramps and linked to the cathedral by a low, inner porch. The three elements, ramp, porch and inner porch, are the formal approach to the nave from the city and they give direction to the circular plan by establishing a strong major axis. The two porches are designed to be both introductory and supporting spaces to the cathedral: that is, their spatial contrasts prepare the visitor for the impact of the vast space of the nave.

A design of large and bold scale was called for if the porch was to hold its own against the powerful forms of the cathedral. Moreover, since bells were required, it seemed obvious that the porch could function as a bell tower if it were high enough to enable the bells to send their message out to the city.

The porch is designed to present a flat vertical front face to the cathedral approaches from the city (72), with the rear face sloping upwards in the opposite direction to the nave roof, to meet the front in a triangular, wedge-shaped section, which is pierced to hold the bells. The design is explained by the section and plan (69–70). The total height is some eighty feet above the podium, which is sufficient for the bells to peal out over the city but far too tall and elongated as an interior space; in consequence, the interior is bisected by an inclined plane into two triangular spaces, the lower being the porch space and the upper housing the bell mechanism. The ceiling planes are kept apart at their apex, leaving a narrow slit which lights the plane facing the entrance, and leaves the opposite plane in shadow. A deep beam spanning the wide opening to the inner porch is designed as a recess for a freize of sculpture facing the entrance and below this beam is a narrower glazed slot which is taken down to the floor on either side, thus dissociating the two porches and providing additional light.

The lower porch is a simple, rectangular substructure inside the podium, with the staircase and lift as visual links between levels. To preserve the rectangular plan, the lift is in a free-standing reinforced concrete cylinder which rises through an open well in the floor, with the top sheared off at an angle to reflect the sloping ceiling above (84). As normal lift mechanism would have made the cylinder excessively tall, the lift is operated hydraulically: there is a ram under the floor and a pump adjacent to the lower part.

The stair is in a rectangular well against a flank wall which, extending from one floor to the other, becomes a linking plane between the two spaces. The stairs have pre-cast treads finished with grey terrazzo and the balustrades are 1 in. diameter tubes, finished a dull black, carrying a flat nickel silver handrail.

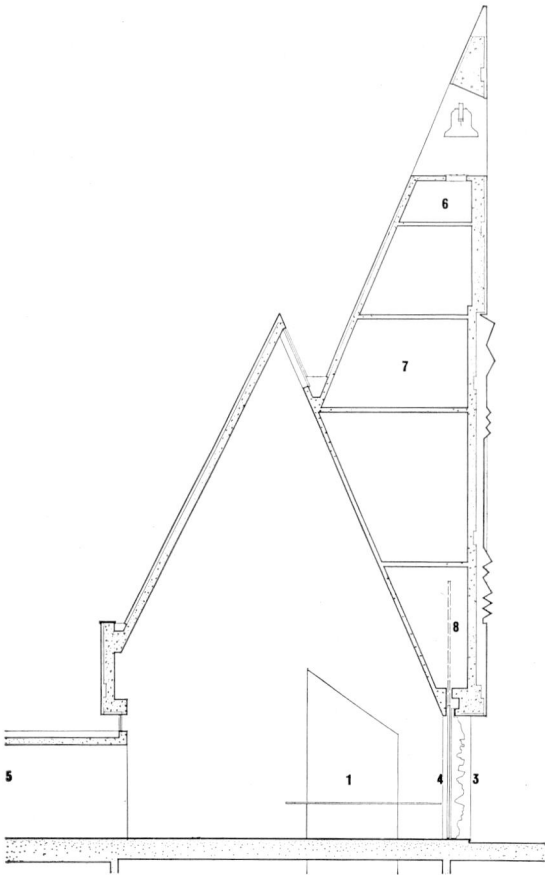

69. Section of main
entrance porch and bell
tower

Key:
1. Lift to lower porch
2. Stair
3. Sliding bronze doors
4. Inner glass screen with
lifting panel
5. Inner connecting porch
6. Bell motor
7. Water tanks
8. Guillotine door gear

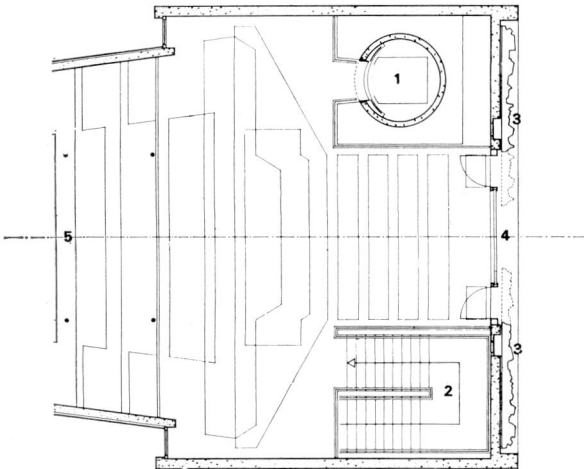

0 ___ 20ft

70. Plan of porch at nave level

71. Floor design by
David Atkins for lower
level of porch

72. *Porch and bell tower from the main approach along Hope Street; the buildings at the front of the porch and adjacent baptistery, will one day be removed*

The colour combination is subdued and in contrast to the strong luminous blues of the nave: the two tent-like ceiling planes and the lift tower are very dark in tone, the vertical flank walls white and the glass framing the connecting porch clear yellow. The grey and white marble floor is integral with that of the nave but downstairs the floor is a simple geometric pattern of dark brickwork – the only decorative element in this simple connecting space to the car park: the picture, (71) is David Atkins' painting of the design.

The building thus composed of a series of flat planes is designed as a homogeneous reinforced concrete structure. My apprehensions about atmospheric pollution led to the concrete being faced externally with a veneer of Portland stone slabs which, with the triangulated shape and absence of windows, gives the building the solid quality of sculptured form.

The carved crosses

The Portland stone veneer simplified the provision of the sculpture on the flat plane of the front elevation: to have cast the concrete against a moulded surface would have complicated the construction and I have an aversion to applied sculpture – 'costume jewellery', as Henry Moore calls it – with the stone veneer it was a simple carving problem. My ideas about the subject matter were vaguely connected with a symbolic reference to crowns: I was not even sure whether the whole thing might not be trite and the only conviction I had was that it must be on a very large and bold scale to be of any significance in the environment. There was, too, the problem of cost; an immense 'hand done' sculpture could have swallowed up funds badly needed for more essential works.

I chose William Mitchell for the job because he works in a bold, direct manner, with a fine sense of materials and no inhibitions about substituting machine technology for handcraft. He came forward with a symbolic design based on three crosses and three crowns (74). The large central cross is surmounted by a crown of thorns and is marked by nail studs and connected to the adjacent crosses by the three crowns, symbols of the dedication to Christ the King. The flanking crosses bear labels: one is plain, whilst the other is intricately carved, symbolic of the silent thief and the forgiven thief who spoke to Our Lord from the cross.

Mitchell produced over a hundred full-size drawings showing exactly how each stone was to be carved, which were then issued to the masonry firm responsible for all the Portland stone at the cathedral. They made a large-scale model to check details and help their men visualise the overall

73. *Facing page: the carved crosses of the bell tower, and the bronze doors slid back*

74. *Below left: William Mitchell's maquette for the carved crosses*

75. *Mr. Horace Davies carving part of the design*

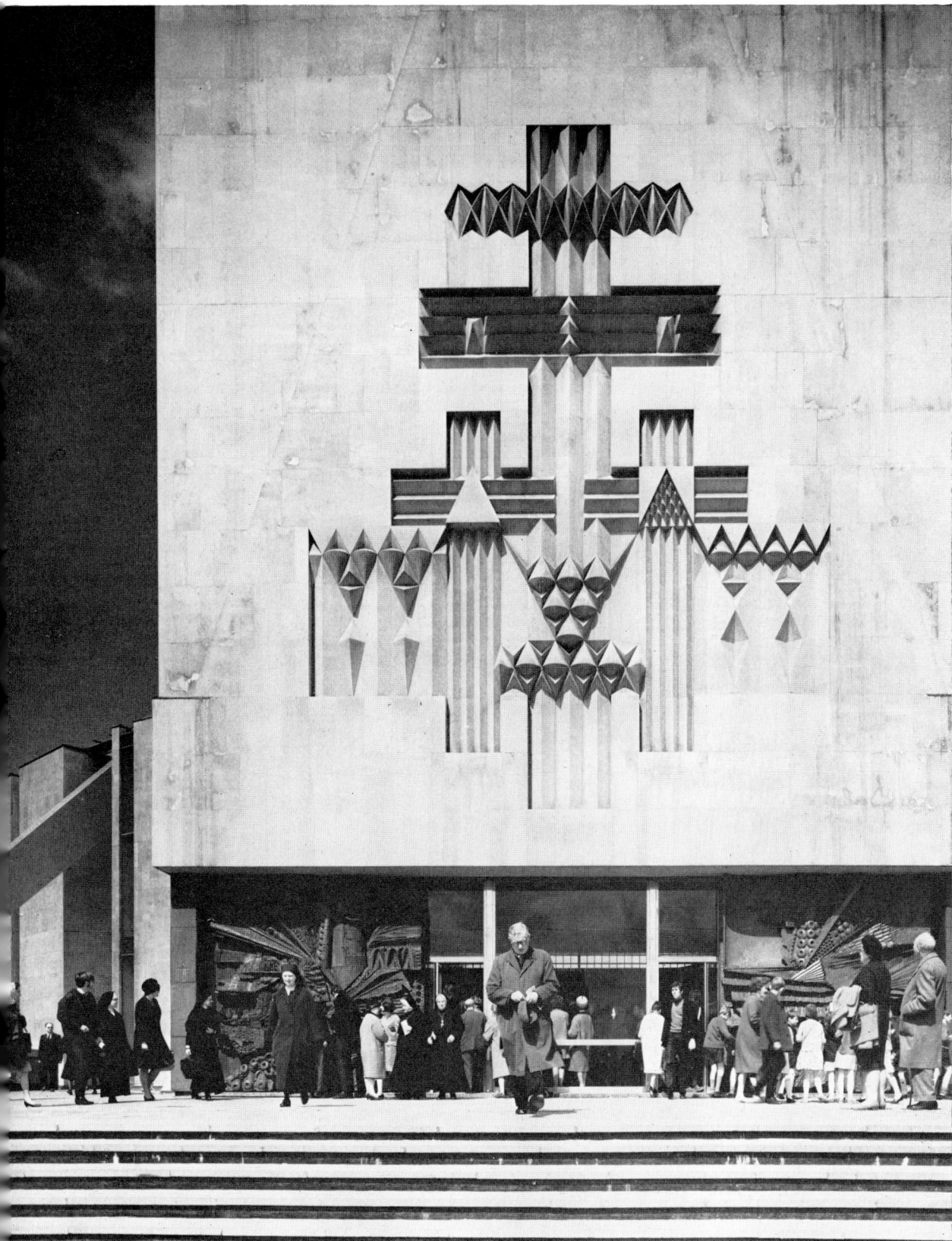

conception and the stone was then cut by machine and by hand – there was more hand carving than I had envisaged, probably because of the complexity of the design – one of the masons, Horace Davies, is shown carving the stone across the foot of the central cross (75).

The stone was not limited in depth to the four inches necessary for the veneer but was brought forward or recessed as required by Mitchell's bold modelling. Altogether 127 stones were carved and some idea of the scale can be gained from the heaviest stones which were at least 6 ft. by 4 ft. and weighed three tons.

The entrance doors

There are two sets of doors to the main entrance: outer bronze-faced solid doors, which are normally kept open; and inner doors in the form of a plate glass screen in bronze framing.
The solid doors are twelve feet square, with a relief sculptured by William Mitchell symbolising the four apostles; the doors are designed to slide

76. One panel of William Mitchell's entrance doors: St. Luke's winged ox and the winged man of St. Matthew

back to appear as decorative panels, leaving a twenty-four foot wide clear entrance between them – the composition is of four squares with a total width of forty-eight feet. I had originally intended that the porch should be completely open, to invite the visitor to enter, the cold being kept out by a heat curtain but, as this proved impracticable, there are doors on either side of a twenty-four foot wide plate glass screen. The idea of the latter was to give a clear view of the interior but, on the occasions when large processions enter the cathedral, it can be raised, guillotine fashion, by an electric motor, to disappear into the structure of the bell tower above. Whether the screen is raised or not the visitor, on climbing the entrance ramp, is confronted by a wide entrance, flanked by two dark and powerful forms, between which is a clear view of the porch interior and the nave beyond.

Inasmuch as bronze ecclesiastical doors can be counted amongst man's most beautiful artifacts (Bonannus at Pisa, Andrea Pisano and Ghiberti at the baptistery, Florence, and, in this spelndid tradition, the modern doors by Giacomo Manzu at St. Peter's, Rome), it was the obvious material for Liverpool. Alas, lack of funds made us explore other materials and, in the end, we adopted a composite structure consisting of a metal frame with

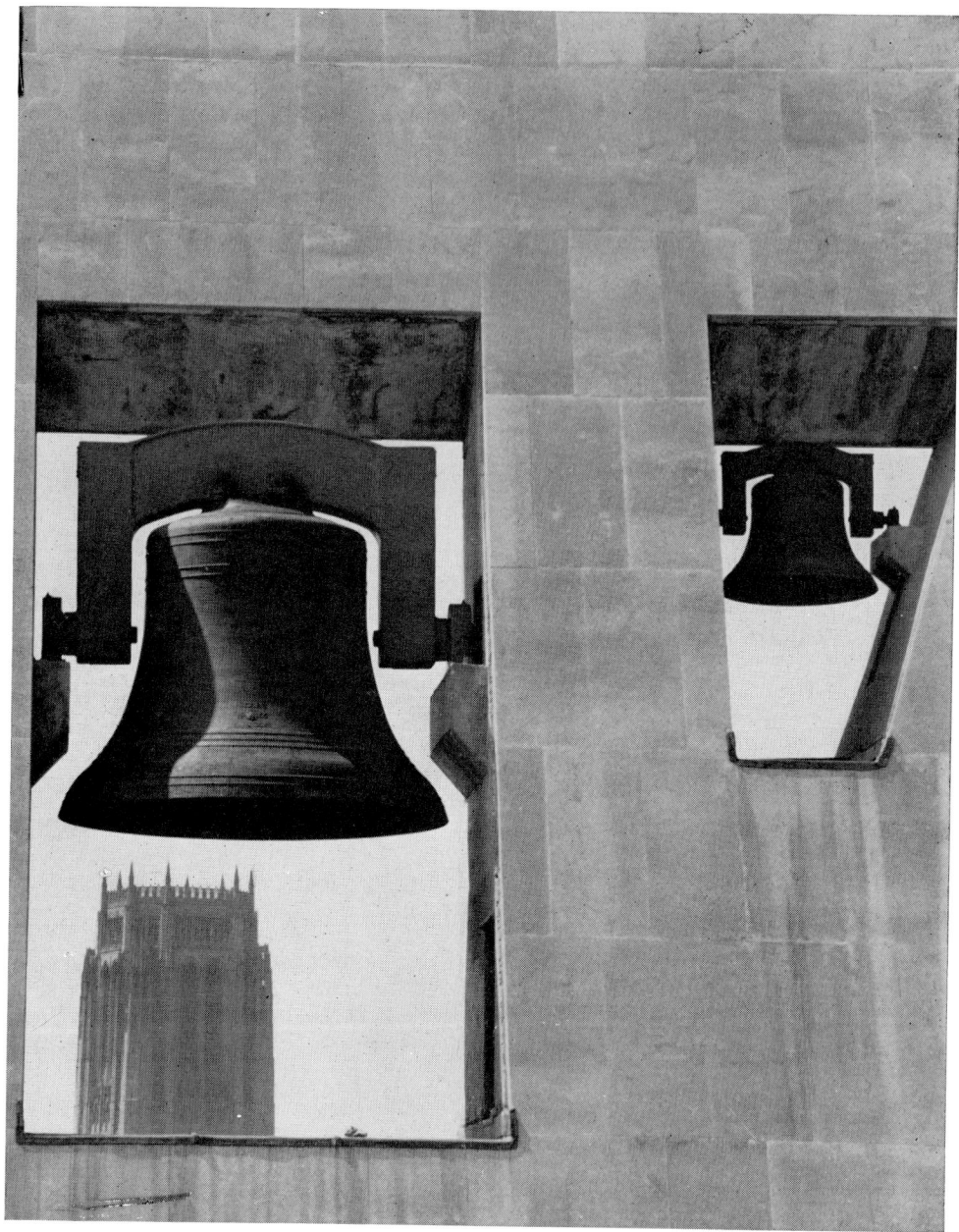

78. Bells Matthew and
John are sixty-nine feet u
to sound across the city

outer and inner skins of bronze-faced fibreglass and a filling of lightweight concrete.

The design for the external face, moulded in great depth, is a free interpretation of the four symbols for the apostles: the left door has the eagle of St. John the Evangelist (which is also the emblem of Christ) and the winged lion of St. Mark; the right door has the winged ox of St. Luke and the winged man, symbol of St. Matthew. The doors were made by first carving polystyrene in a mould and then pouring in a mixture of fibreglass, polyester resin and bronze powder, which latter set as a rock-hard bronze

112

surface. This outer skin was fixed to a steel frame, a core of lightweight concrete poured into it and, finally, the back of fibreglass was bonded on. The doors weigh two tons each and are hung on a sliding track and opened by a geared hand winch inside the porch.

Bells

The entrance doors are intricate and complicated designs which have their maximum impact when seen close to at eye level after climbing the ramp. The bells, on the contrary, attain their greatest significance seen silhouetted in their setting down the long vista of Hope Street.

Each bell is hung in a rectangular opening pierced through the wedge-shaped apex of the porch and lined with stone to provide a simple sculptured setting. The openings are large enough to allow the silhouettes of the bells to be significant and their proportions are related to the size of each individual bell.

The bells were named Matthew, Mark, Luke and John (each has its name cast on it) and they were cast at the Whitechapel Bell Foundry where, since 1570, some of the world's great bells have been cast, such as Great Tom and Great Paul in St. Paul's Cathedral and the bells of Westminster Abbey, originally cast in 1583.

The total weight of the bells, including headstocks and clappers, is nearly ten tons: the individual weights and notes are:

Matthew	A^b	weighing	4 tons 12 cwt.
Mark	E^b	weighing	1 ton 6 cwt.
Luke	A^b	weighing	$10\frac{3}{4}$ cwt.
John	C	weighing	$8\frac{1}{4}$ cwt.

The bells are swung by electric motors housed in a motor room immediately beneath the bells and, in addition, each one can be tolled electrically by a hammer on its outside surface while it is stationary. It is possible to swing or toll any bell singly or in combination with all or any of the others. The bells are controlled from the sacristies, where a switch panel provides individual control, or a set programme which will continue automatically.

The connecting porch

The connecting porch (left in 84) came into being because I wanted the bell tower to be detached so that it would not be confused with the form of the cathedral. Tower and porch underline the principal axis; but the porch is also a vital element in the introductory spaces to the cathedral. It is designed as a wide but exceptionally low space so that, after passing through the tent-like space of the bell tower, the eye is brought down and focussed on the nave beyond.

The walls converge towards the nave and are lit from above by concealed roof lights so that their flat, uninterrupted planes lead the eye onwards. The ceiling is only nine feet high and, in sharp contrast to the light grey of the flanking walls, the colour is a very dark slate grey.

A glass and aluminium screen across the end of the inclined walls insulates the nave from noise, after which the space expands sideways to a chapel on one side and the baptistery on the other and then merges with that of the nave.

79. Chapel of the Blessed Sacrament

114

9. CHAPEL OF THE BLESSED SACRAMENT

The requirement for the tabernacle (a tabernacle is a small cupboard or safe) containing the Blessed Sacrament, the consecrated bread and wine of the Eucharist, was that it should be placed in a separate chapel, from which priests would pass to the high altar carrying the Blessed Sacrament — problems that arise when the tabernacle is associated with the high altar (such as its obstructing the view of the celebrant's actions), did not, therefore, arise. Because of its importance and association with the high altar, the chapel was placed as a termination of the main axis of the cathedral, with a clear view between their respective altars.

This chapel is the largest and the most intricate; its interior expands outwards and upwards towards its own sanctuary to give a character of seclusion and depth. The chapel projects well beyond the others and is wider because its walls close up to the flying buttresses: the problem posed by the integration of the raking lines of the buttresses had a considerable influence on the unusual design of the building.

The plan and section (80–1) explain the design. The side walls follow lines radiating from the centre point of the cathedral, and are terminated by the flat plane of the end wall at right angles to the main axis. The inside face of the end wall forms the background for the sanctuary and, as the building is on the centre line of the piazza, the outside of the end wall forms a setting for the external altar. The seating, for about a hundred people, is in parallel rows; it increases in length as the chapel expands towards the sanctuary and it can extend into the nave space.

Although the entrance to the chapel stretches the full width between the nave columns, the height is restricted by the organ gallery above and so the chapel expands upwards towards its sanctuary, to complement the expanding side walls. The solution devised to express the raking buttresses within the side walls is shown in the diagrammatic section (80). From the low ceiling of the chapel entrance (15 ft. high), a flat roof slab is inclined upwards at an angle of 45°, to meet the end wall; the outside edges of this slab intersect the raking buttresses at right angles and form triangular spaces with the end wall which become the two windows. There is thus a wedge-shaped chapel expanding towards its sanctuary, which is backed by a broad expanse of wall, side-lit by triangular windows adjacent to it.

The sanctuary

The sanctuary extends the full width of the building: the altar is at the front and, behind it, recessed at eye level in the end wall is the tabernacle (85). To reconcile the big difference in scale between the tabernacle and the rectangular wall a picture, or reredos, some twenty feet long by nine feet high, is recessed in the wall over the tabernacle. There is an unusual,

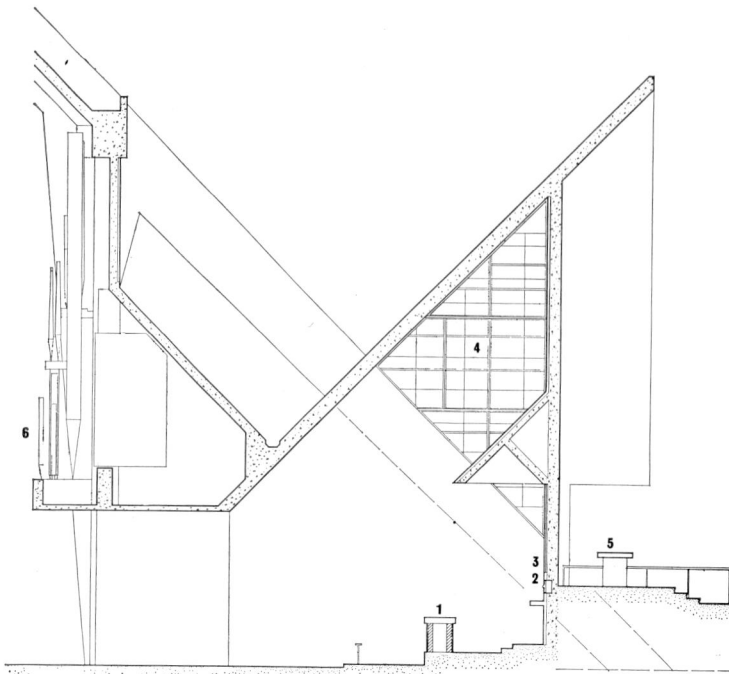

80. Section of chapel of
the Blessed Sacrament

Key:
1. Altar
2. Tabernacle
3. Reredos
4. Stained glass windows
5. External altar
6. Organ

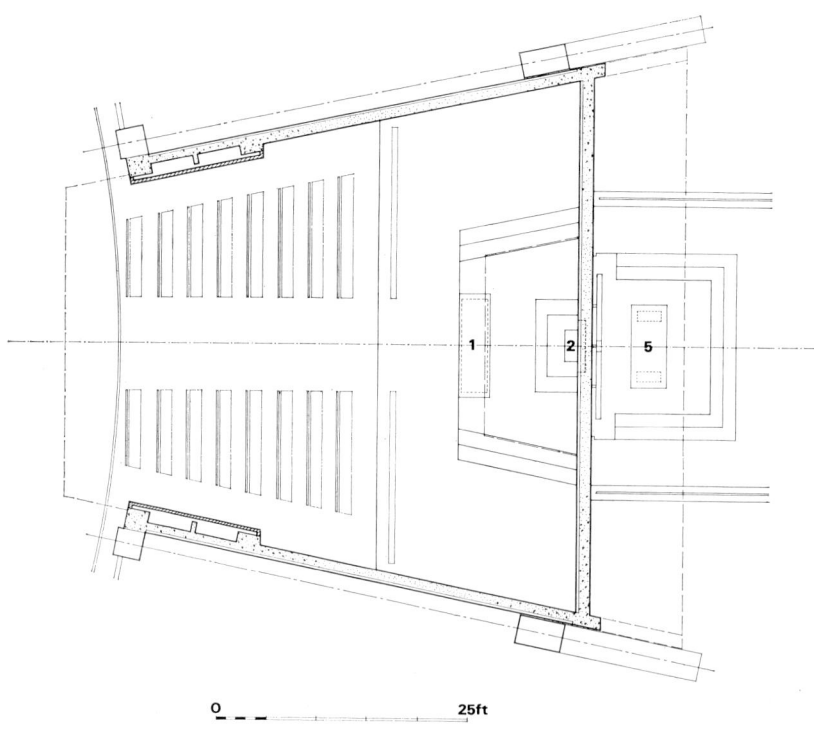

81. Plan of chapel of the
Blessed Sacrament

O _ _ _ _____ 25ft

probably unique condition of four interacting elements: a large, painted
reredos related to flanking stained glass windows at right angles to it, with
a comparatively small element, the tabernacle, as the focus of the composition.

I hoped that the liturgical requirement that the altar and tabernacle   116 should be covered by a canopy could be waived, because of its possible interference with the sloping roof plane but, as this was not possible, I placed a kind of hood over it, in the form of a reinforced concrete slab inclined from the wall, at the same 45° angle as the ceiling and supported at each end by triangular brackets. As the canopy is homogeneous with the wall, it is faced on the outside with the same stone but, to avoid it being too thick and clumsy, the inside is lined with white mosaic.

The predella is raised by three steps above the floor of the sanctuary and the plain altar of white marble is placed in line with the edge of the predella. Behind the altar, against the rear wall, a step gives access to the tabernacle which is above the altar, to be in sight of the congregation.

The spatial triptych

The two windows with the reredos between them form a single composition across the space of the sanctuary, with the tabernacle as the focus: they are a kind of spatial triptych. Two quite different mediums are worked in their design: oil paint on board and coloured glass in lead cames.

All the cathedral windows are of abstract design – they no longer need to be coloured picture books for an illiterate mediaeval congregation – so it seemed to me that the painting must also be abstract and by the same artist, otherwise they would become dissociated. But this abstract painting was not required for its own sake – a cathedral is not an art gallery – but is there to assist devotion. Few artists could have tackled so difficult a problem but I had no doubts that it was made for Ceri Richards. He had already done some stained glass designs and so there were no fears that the technique would be alien to him; as to the painting, the *Cathédrale Engloutie* series, in which he take for his subject Debussy's piano prelude on the legend of the drowned cathedral of Ys, were proof enough that he was capable of evoking profound liturgical associations through a great work of art. And so it has turned out to be.

Now that we have no common culture, it is inevitable that the commissioning of any work of art is fraught with difficulties and frustrations – even more so with the Church; look at the wares displayed in any ecclesiastical shop. Small wonder I had some apprehension in broaching the subject with the Cathedral Committee. Basil Spence has told of the Coventry Cathedral Committee's stunned incomprehension of the work of Graham Sutherland; my Committee, although not exactly stunned with the work of Ceri Richards, were singularly lacking in enthusiasm: but at least Archbishop Beck expressed a wish to visit Ceri Richards' studio. This he accordingly did, not once but three times and eventually decided to recommend to the Committee that the work be commissioned – I had, on my own initiative, already commissioned sketch designs for the reredos and Patrick Reyntiens gave enthusiastic support, both as a Catholic and an artist.

The three designs were developed simultaneously by Ceri Richards in his studio and, after they had been finally agreed, the tabernacle was made by Wauthier Osborne Guild Ltd., the windows by Patrick Reyntiens and the artist painted the reredos in the Tate Gallery, where a room was made available to him.

The tabernacle

Although the tabernacle is unusually large – 5 ft. long and 1 ft. 6 in. high – so that it can contain all the ciboria needed for the most important feast days, it is nevertheless a small object within the context of the chapel. On the other hand, it is the most sacred object in the whole cathedral and should command attention and reverence. It must also be as strong as any safe or place of safe keeping for the Blessed Sacrament.

It is constructed of steel fixed in a recess in the reinforced concrete wall of the chapel, and the design enriches the three locked doors which give access to the interior. The design is intricate in colour and texture and Ceri Richards made full use of the experience of Wauthier Osborne Guild Limited and their craftsmen in the use of decorative materials. The centre door, used on most occasions, symbolises the glory of God by representing the heavens and constellations. It has a base of silver and bronze plate filled with coloured enamel and polished brass, over which is mounted cast brass, $\frac{1}{4}$ in. blue optical glass, opal and green glass and ivory. The doors on either side symbolise the Passion and depict in simple form the chalice and the cross and, here again, the design is built up with rich materials on a background of silver and bronze plates.

The reredos and windows

The reredos (82) and windows are an abstract design in pale keys of yellows and blues, suggesting a mysterious infinity of cool space. The geometric design of the reredos is complemented by the free flowing curves of the stained glass and, in certain lights, the rear wall of the chapel and the painting are stained by blues and yellows from the windows.

The painting, in oil, is exceptionally large, 20 ft. by 8 ft. 6 in. and because of the problems of durability, resistance to atmospheric change and trans-

82. Facing page, top: the Blessed Sacrament chapel, showing one of flanking windows, the reredos and tabernacle, all designed by Ceri Richards, which togeth form the spatial triptyc. 83. Bottom left: the baptistery gates by Da Atkins. 84. Bottom right: the main and lower porch and the dr enclosing the lift. The way into the cathedral to the left

85. The tabernacle doors

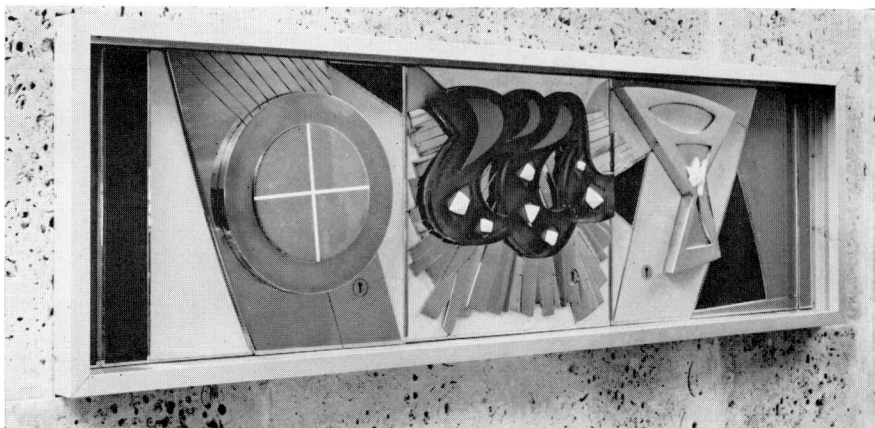

port, it was painted on three primed, 1-in. thick laminated wood boards, each weighing two hundredweight. The boards interlock and are mounted in the recess, fixed by a narrow anodised aluminium frame.

The windows presented the most complex problems in which structural engineering and the design, techniques and limitations of glass manufacture were inextricably interwoven.

From the artist's design drawings were prepared to show the pattern of thin lines that would be introduced by the lead cames linking the individual pieces of glass, and the thicker lines of the steel framing required to support the glass against the wind. The position of the lead cames and the steel framing were influenced by the need to preserve the free and flowing outlines of the original design and were dimensioned to the last $\frac{1}{16}$ in. The full-size cartoons were then prepared jointly by the artist and Patrick Reyntiens, who made the glass, sizes being carefully checked by my office.

Each window is divided into seven separate steel frames of varying shape, the largest with intermediate members to further reduce the area of unsupported glass. As soon as each frame was complete, hardboard templates were made to exact size and sent to Patrick Reyntiens. Against the full-size cartoons, the templates were marked with the position of the glazing beads on the outer edges and intermediately, so that these followed exactly the line of the lead cames. The templates were then returned to the steelwork fabricator in Liverpool and the grilles of glazing beads were welded. The final operation was the fixing of the steelwork on site and then the glazing.

The lines of cames and structural frames, although part of the design, become a minor supporting element as the colours and forms of the design rise above them in brilliance (79).

10. THE LADY CHAPEL

The Lady Chapel, like the Chapel of the Blessed Sacrament, is a self-contained architectural composition, projecting well beyond the other chapels but differing in that the interior space is fully open to the nave. The building is adjacent to the west porch with its altar on a major axis struck from the centre of the sanctuary.

My conception of the building was of a tall, narrow light space of extreme refinement and quiet elegance, using materials of cool colours and a wide range of smooth textures, from soft fabrics to hard marble.

The plan form (89) is, at a first glance, complex but it will be clarified if seen as a reconciliation of the circular nave space, of which it forms an extension, and the rectangular podium on which it stands. The side walls of the building radiate from the centre point of the cathedral and are terminated by two end walls parallel to the edges of the rectangular podium and meeting at right angles to form a triangular space, which is the sanctuary. The building thus expands towards the sanctuary, in the opposite direction to the high altar. The seating, for ninety-four people, increases in length the closer it is to the sanctuary and it can extend into the nave of the cathedral.

To avoid this complicated geometric space becoming confused, the walls are designed as flat planes with reinforced concrete columns within them: but the structure reveals itself in the high ceiling, as a triangular pattern of deep concrete beams supporting a flat concrete roof slab.

A deep dado (7 ft. 6 in. high) of white Sicilian marble extends round all the walls and above, to the underside of the roof, tall, narrow windows with oak reveals alternate with narrow panels of raw silk.

The sanctuary

The altar is placed at the centre of gravity of the triangular shape of the sanctuary and well above, in the apex of the triangle, is a large madonna and child, supported on a cantilevered shelf. This sculpture was chosen by the Cathedral Committee from four maquettes submitted by Robert Brumby and is made of terracotta left in its natural warm red-brown colour. Because of its size, (9 ft. high), it was cast and baked in three sections and jointed together in the chapel. As a cool background to the sculpture, the sanctuary walls are faced with white mosaic.

The sanctuary is lit by a glass spire over the altar, square on plan with two sides parallel to the two rear walls. It has a bronze frame and the apex, which extends into a finial, is filled with bronze panels.

86. *Lady Chapel*

Stained glass

In contrast to the robust concrete and glass technique used for the tower, the windows of the Lady Chapel are of thin glass with lead cames, held in narrow section bronze frames, with reveals of waxed, polished, light English oak. The design by Margaret Traherne is of simplicity and refinement and is based on a geometric motif with a colour range from milky white to warm amber. The windows behind the sanctuary have warm tones at the bottom, fading to cooler tones at the top; this sequence is reversed in the other windows.

The glass is thin, hand-made, glass of antique type, jointed by lead cames. Considerable variations within each sheet play an important part in the overall effect. The glass was specially manufactured in Germany and is flashed with a thin film of opalescent white over three basic colours: a warm white, a light amber and a deep amber. The repeat motif is formed on the glass by removing the white film to reveal areas of base

123

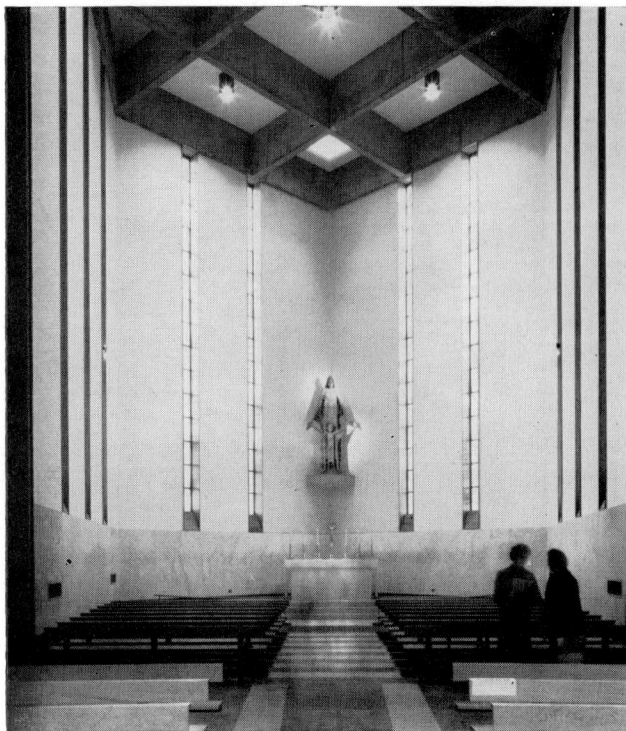

*87. Interior of Lady
Chapel, showing
Madonna and child by
Robert Brumby*

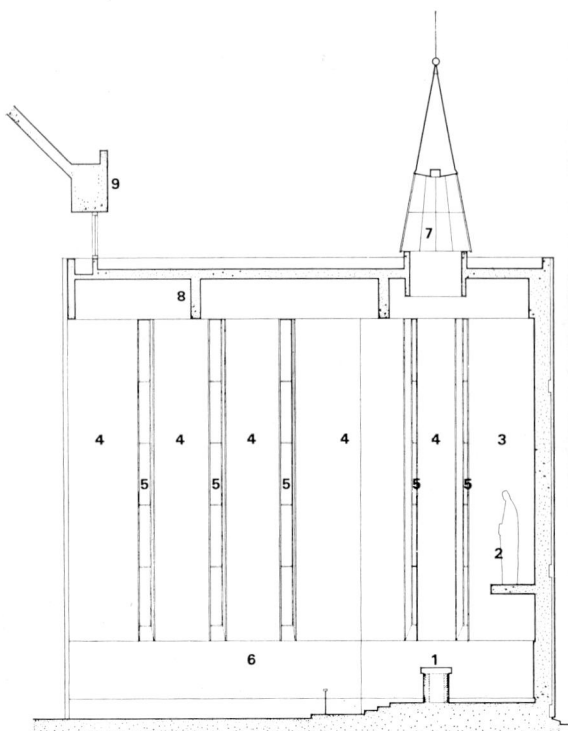

*88. Section of Lady
Chapel*

Key:
1. Altar
2. Terracotta madonna
   statue
3. Mosaic
4. Silk wall hangings
5. Engraved glass
6. Sicilian marble
7. Bronze lantern
8. Concrete beams
9. Lower ring beam

*89. Plan of Lady
Chapel*

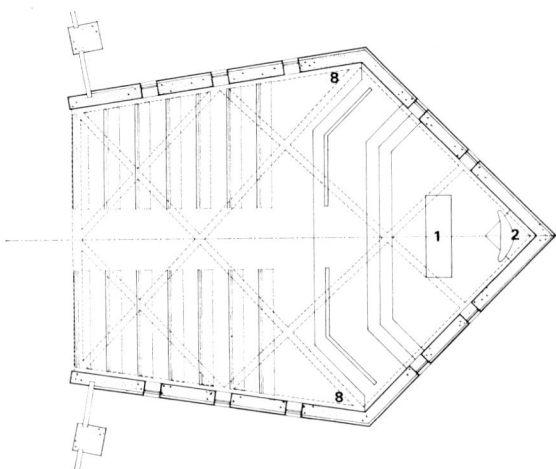

O _ . _ 20ft

glass. The motif and the base, or ground, are acid-etched in alter-
nation, to give a fluctuating movement between warm opalescence and
barely-diffused colour within the general change from light to dark in
each window.

11. THE CHAPELS OF SAINTS

It will be clear by now that the small chapels surrounding the nave are among the most significant elements of the total design. Not before has a cathedral been enclosed by a series of buildings which, independent in both designs and construction, are yet interlocked with the total space and the total structural form.

There are eight small chapels which, although diverse in their forms, all have the same basic shape in which the side walls radiate from the centre of the cathedral, and the front and back walls are arcs of circles struck from the same centre point (91). In height they are all contained by a flat roof slab, the top of which is 45 ft. above the floor, leaving a foot-wide clerestorey above. Each, as we have seen, is a free-standing, load-bearing brick structure, in places reinforced by concrete and faced on the outside with Portland stone. I had wished to extend this stone finish past the stained glass windows into the nave, so that the inner core was contained by the same outer skin, but the restricted amount of money available made this impossible. As it is, the walls inside the nave are faced with buff cement render which, although distinct in appearance from the adjacent concrete column, has nothing like the same variety of texture and density as stone – compare the end wall of the Chapel of the Blessed Sacrament. When the chapels are enclosed they have their own individual wall treatment.

The competition conditions gave no lead to the character of the chapels, all that was asked for was: "about eight side altars in small chapels, with seating for about twelve people". My design intention was that, whereas all the chapels should have an intimacy and intricacy, in contrast to the vast space of the nave, there should be a variety of individual designs, from comparatively tiny hollowed-out rooms into which one may retire in absolute seclusion, to open spaces which form extensions of the nave (48).

The methods of obtaining diversity between the chapels are several. Firstly, through the placing of the altar; the majority have the altar on the centre of the rear wall which is on an axis of the centre of the building, and therefore is a focus from the nave. Some of these altars are set in re-cesses, which modify the external form of the building; and some are brought forward towards the nave space. The altars in two of the chapels are placed against an end wall, at a right angle to the axis, making them almost invisible from the nave. One of these, the largest (St. Thomas of Canterbury), has an entrance from the main porch, so that it may be completely independent – a characteristic which has given it the sad fate of acting as a temporary bookshop.

A second broad way in which diversity has arisen is in the effective floor area, which dictates the seating capacity. In order to keep the nave space absolutely clear of incidental forms, all the special equipment is

90. East porch, chapels of St. Thomas Aquinas and St. Columba and a stair tower

within the chapels: thus, the confessionals are placed in three of them, giving enclosure from the nave, (9), staircases or stores reduce the length of three others, and space is also needed for ducts conveying such services as electricity – the floor measurements range from the 28 ft. by 18 ft., seating 45, to 18 ft. square, which is most suited for solitary prayer. There is, too, considerable variation in the heights of the buildings: in particular two of them, on the east and west sides, are designed to provide television galleries covering the whole of the sanctuary.

The quality of the space itself has, of course, given the most emphatic distinctions in character. The shape of the volume, how the volume relates to the altar, the direction and quality of the light and the degree to which the space is allowed to merge with the nave, are all critical elements in the individuality of each chapel.

The Cathedral Committee decided the dedication of each chapel. Beginning adjacent to the east stair tower and anti-clockwise round the building they are as follows: St. Joseph, St. Anne, St. Paul of the Cross St. Thomas of Canterbury, St. George and English Martyrs, St. Patrick, St. Thomas Aquinas and St. Columba.

A fund was started for each of the chapels and, at the time of the consecration, two of them, St. Joseph (No. 3) and St. Paul of the Cross (No. 5), were completed; and one, St. Thomas of Canterbury (No. 6), was being used as a temporary bookshop. The remaining five though left as plain shells, are equipped with altars, so that they may be used, – I am not, as some have supposed, disappointed that these buildings have not been realised; on the contrary, I like to think of future generations being able to embellish and develop the cathedral over the years.

Although five of the chapels are bare shells, it was necessary to glaze them to keep the wet out and, rather than use temporary plain glass, which would have been a violent contrast with the coloured nave, it was decided that the stained glass should be commissioned. David Atkins designed the Chapel of St. Thomas Aquinas in thin English antique glass. The narrow horizontal windows on the flank walls are in a rose colour range and the tall windows on either side of the altar are in subdued colours in a geo-

126

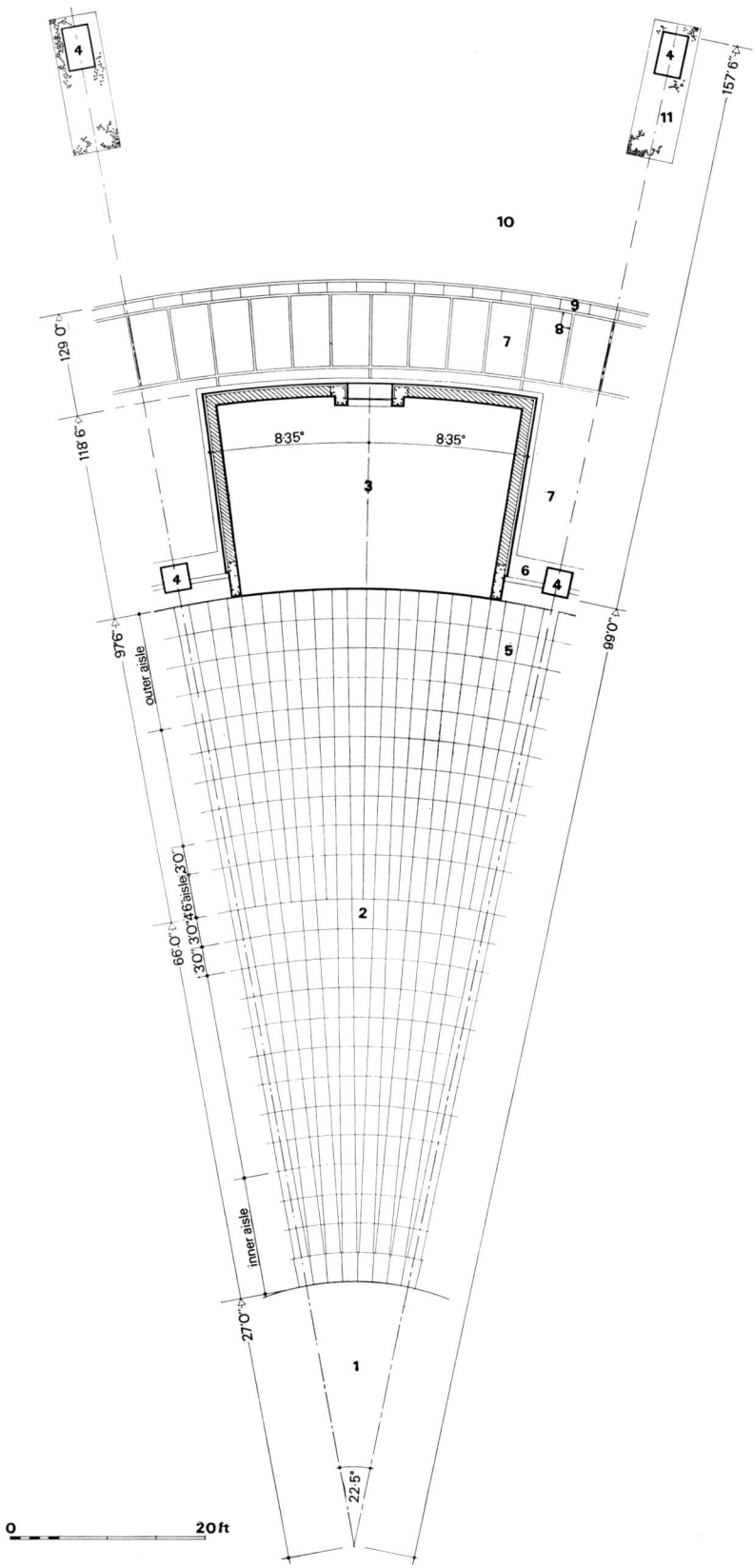

91. *Plan showing the
setting-out of chapels in
relation to the centre
point of the cathedral*

Key:
1. *Sanctuary*
2. *Nave*
3. *Chapel*
4. *Main structural frame*
5. *Marble paving*
6. *Slate plinth*
7. *Brushed concrete*
8. *Slate slip joints*
9. *Curved cast iron grating*
10. *Random slate paving*
11. *Cobble panel round
main frame*

127

metric progression. He also did the chapel of St. Columba, again in thin glass, where the twenty-three small square windows form a pattern of juxtaposed crimson and purple.

John Piper and Patrick Reyntiens were responsible for the chapels of St. Anne, and St. George and the English Martyrs, in thick cast glass of similar design. They also did the windows of the staircase towers on either side of the entrance to the Chapel of the Blessed Sacrament. These are a repeat design but the predominant colour on one side of the chapel is green and, on the other side, red, which I find upsetting to the symmetry of the building.

Chapel of St. Joseph

The chapel is adjacent to the Lady Chapel and was designed to be one of the smallest and most intimate in the cathedral. Its character is that of an enclosed funnel-like space, the head of which provides the sole source of light and directs it to a free-standing altar. The chapel is roughly 18 ft. square on plan, the rest of the building accommodating a tall store for ladders. The square plan is extended vertically, first by walls faced with pine boarding, for a height of 12 ft. and then by a hard, white, fibrous plaster pyramid which is reduced at the top to a narrow neck, surmounted by a roof light some 45 ft. above floor level.

Everything is subordinated to the centrally-placed altar and its free-standing predella, both of which are in grey Burlington slate surrounded by the floor of dark brindle quarry tiles. From the nave the altar is seen, bathed in white light, through a wide opening above which is a tall niche with sloping rear wall and heavy concrete base. This niche reflects the shape of the pyramid, (its outside face, so to speak), and its purpose is to provide a setting for a massive memorial by some future Thornhill or Bernini.

Chapel of St. Paul of the Cross

The chapel is on the west side of the nave, midway between the main entrance and side porches. The space is open to the nave and the design is symmetrical about a line struck from the centre of the cathedral, on which line is placed the altar, against the rear wall. Above the altar is a tall window extending the full height of the building, from which the chapel largely draws its identity. At eye level, the space is screened from the nave by confessionals, between which the entrance is formed by concrete enclosing walls and lintol.

The window, 30 ft. high by 2 ft. 6 in. wide, is clearly visible from the nave and was designed and made by Margaret Traherne. The glass is of a thin, handmade antique type fixed in lead cames, giving it a lighter, more limpid quality than the cast nave glass. The colours range from red to rose, the colour of martyrdom and fire, the deepest tones being the lowest (earthly) level. The first impression from the nave is of a pattern of beautifully proportioned coloured rectangles; then one sees that they trace out a large Latin cross and that they form a series of ladders: in Margaret Traherne's words, "instruments of Passion and for their part in the deposition of Christ. They are relevant to the visions of St. Paul of the Cross and the order of Passionists which he founded."

All the other elements are subordinate to this splendid window and the white marble altar beneath it – in certain lights the whole chapel is a glowing red. The ceiling is white plaster, the walls buff cement render, the confessionals waxed oak and the floor extends the grey and white marble of the nave.

12. THE BAPTISTERY

After the high altar and the tabernacle, the Catholic church regards the baptismal font as the most sacred object in the church. "It houses the consecrated water and is the scene of the Christian regeneration and of incorporation into the mystical Body of Christ*." Such a place must obviously have its own spatial setting which clearly distinguishes it from other areas: this is most powerfully done when it is given the self-contained space of a baptistery. Such was the requirement for Liverpool, where it was specified that there should be a baptistery near the entrance and of about five hundred square feet floor area. This traditional arrangement (in so far as there is a tradition for a rite which originally involved total immersion in any convenient stretch of water†), means that the sacrament begins in the porch, continues in the church outside the entrance to the baptistery and is concluded at the font.

Clearly Liverpool rejected a modern tendency to regard the sacrament of baptism, or re-birth, as being one which involves the whole seated congregation and not merely a group of relatives and friends. For this to happen it is necessary for the font to be a liturgical focus in the nave or hall of worship, which sets difficult design problems in a Catholic church, as it cannot be associated with the altar, as has been the case with some nonconformist churches. Had the cathedral been a parish church, then the baptistery might well have been a room or narthex large enough to accommodate the whole standing congregation. But it is not, it is a cathedral, which, in accordance with cathedral tradition, has a baptistery: so it seemed to me that the most desirable arrangement was to place the building immediately adjacent to the main porch, from which the font could be glimpsed, but to open it to the nave so that its area could be extended. This position also had advantages to the external views as, being prominent from the city approach, the building is a reminder that Christian life begins with baptism and proceeds to the altar – symbolised by the tower rising behind it.

The cylindrical space

As the rite of baptism requires the people to gather round the priest and the child, the most appropriate building form is one in which the space is developed outwards and upwards from a central font, (92–3).

A font is a bowl: bowls are normally circular on plan – which suggested that the space containing it should also be circular – the traditional octagon is just as appropriate but it would have been an uncomfortable

---

* J. O'Connell, *Church Building and Furnishing*, Burns Oates & Washbourne.

† Article 'Baptismal Architecture' by J. G. Davies in Lockett, *The Modern Architectural Setting of the Liturgy*, S.P.C.K.

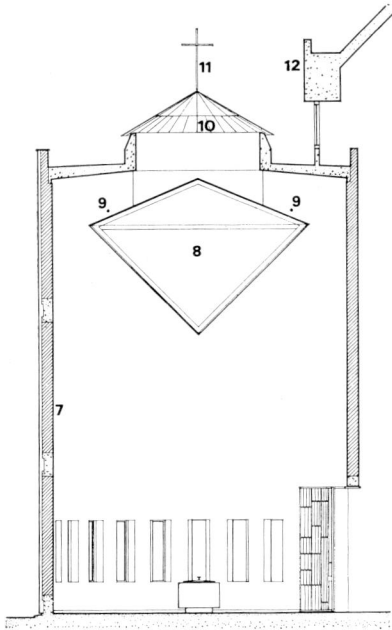

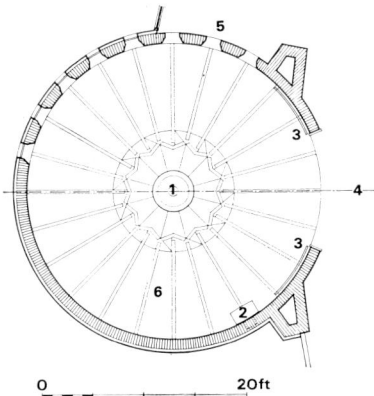

93. Section of baptistery

form between my flying buttresses. From the circular plan the building is developed as a cylindrical drum with the font in the centre and a wide opening to the nave: the font, the opening to the nave and the high altar are on a common axis.

The drum is pierced by small rectangular openings at eye level, to give a glimpse of the font from the porch before one enters the nave, and the pattern of the openings is extended by windows, making a regular progression for about a third of the circumference.

To underline the cylindrical drum-like form, the natural lighting was designed to illuminate the walls without revealing the source of light. This is done by a glazed circular lantern or skylight, set in the flat roof and obscured from view by a conical form which is suspended over the font and which deflects the light on to the wall surfaces – the cone might be likened to the canopy which sometimes surmounts the font in large baptisteries, albeit I was unaware of this practice when I designed it. As can

131

be seen on the sectional drawing (92), the cone points downwards to the centre of the font but, to my surprise, optical illusion changes the cone into a hemisphere and there is no sense of direction between the apex of the cone and the font.

To give the cylindrical form its maximum significance, the walls are a continuous surface of slightly-textured white paint: an idea I had of incising in the plaster some appropriate text in splendid lettering was dismissed by the Committee, no doubt rightly so, as being irrelevant.

As the building has a unique liturgical function, the floor breaks away from the overall grey and white marble of the rest of the cathedral. The design (93), again by David Atkins, radiates from the font in the form of thin lines of black marble set in a light grey terrazzo. Towards the centre and relating to the ends of the black lines, are slightly darker grey terrazzo triangles and intersecting rectangles which define a circle.

The building is clad outside with the same Portland stone slabs used for the chapels and its conical roof light, constructed of bronze and rough cast glass, is surmounted by a tall bronze cross. The elongated cylindrical form rising from the raised podium is prominent from the approach roads and ramp to the cathedral entrance (94).

The font

Several attempts were made to design the font (95) before a form was found that satisfied the Committee. There were no problems with the base (any solid structure is allowable) and so I used the same white marble as the altar, in the form of a drum – the logical shape for people to gather round. The diameter is large (4 ft.), to prevent it getting too crowded and to be in scale with the baptistery space. The difficulty was with the water container, or containers, for two bowls are required: one, the smaller, for the baptismal water; and the other to receive the water after it has been sprinkled on the infant. The bowls are required to have a tight-fitting cover with a lock, to preserve the water from dust and "any profane or superstitious use". The placing of these unequal bowls within the circle of the base and covered with a large lid only seemed to result in unsatisfactory shapes, in which were left large areas of marble top of no practical use. Moreover, the two bowls, by dictating the position of the child, gave the plan a direction, undesirable in a circular space. I finally put to the Committee the idea of a bowl within a bowl: that is, a central deep bowl of small diameter holding about seven pints of holy water, surrounded by a continuous shallow trough, so that the font could be used from any position. The whole is slightly below the flat marble outer rim, which is sufficiently wide for the things used at baptism to be laid on it.

The font cover is a simple shallow, dished lid, made of silver-plated brass. Unlike some of the font covers in the great cathedrals, it is not so heavy that it has to be suspended from above; so I was denied the pleasures of exploring the mechanics of pulleys and their aesthetic expression.

94. Baptistery

95. The font, glimpsed
from the connecting porch

The gates

Baptisteries are required to be locked by gates or grilles and at Liverpool this problem was complicated by the wide opening being curved on plan. Gates hung on hinges, in the ordinary way, would intrude on the room when folded back (because the curve of the gate is in the opposite direction to that of the wall): so they are hung from a track, to slide back on either side against the walls of the baptistery.

The Liverpool City Council offered £2,000 to the cathedral fund and it was agreed that it should be spent on the baptistery gates – this sum may sound a paltry gift from so great a city but they also helped finance the opening festival. The cost limit precluded any spectacular example of the metalworkers' art; compared with John Tresilian's chantry gates at St. George's Chapel, Windsor, or those of William Edney in the nave of St. Mary Redcliffe, Bristol, David Atkins' gates at Liverpool are modest in the extreme; nonetheless, they are designs of deceptive refinement and subtlety.

The gates (83), consist of a flat, rectangular, bronze frame sub-divided into very tall rectangular panels, into which are set vertical flat brass members which are inclined towards the interior – rather like venetian blinds on end. The effect of this inclination, which differs between panels, is to fragment the view from the nave into the baptistery: moreover, due to the curve on the gates, the view changes as one moves across the opening to the baptistery. Although each gate appears to have a different pattern they are, in fact, identical, one being hung in the reverse direction to the other. The formal interest is heightened by the contrast in light refraction between brass and bronze and between inclined planes against curved.

13. THE EAST AND WEST PORCHES

The east and west porches establish the secondary axis of the cathedral: externally they form the focus of the views from the piazza approach and staircases and internally they provide stepped galleries or tribunes looking down on to the sanctuary.

The entrance porch itself is low with a dark ceiling so that, on entry, the view is first concentrated on to the high altar and then extends upwards and outwards into the body of the nave space.

The design is explained in the plans and section (97–9): the centre of the building extends upwards, well above the roof level of the other buildings, to mark its importance, and takes the form of a hood designed to deflect light, through a glass roof light down into the gallery, and to form the background of a free-standing bronze cross (96).

The entrance is surmounted by a very deep lintol faced with slate, over which are a recess which will one day contain a sculpture group, and two narrow stained glass windows extending the full height of the building.

96. The east porch. Below it is the entrance to a sacristy. The building in the right foreground is the presbytery

There are two sets of entrance doors, the outer bronze-faced and the inner glazed, arranged to form an entrance lobby. The solid doors are normally kept open, each six-foot wide leaf being hinged to fold back and form the side walls of the porches.

The outer doors, by William Mitchell, are of similar construction to the main entrance doors, each having a steel frame with bronze-impregnated fibreglass fronts and backs and an inner filling of vermiculite and resin. The glass inner doors are held in anodised aluminium framing.

Access to the galleries is from staircases in the porches, so that they are independent of the nave; the staircase to the east porch also continues down to the sacristies below. The staircases are in concrete finished with pre-cast terrazzo and have simple balustrades of mild steel standards, painted black and carrying a silver-bronze handrail.

The stepped galleries cantilever three feet into the nave, with a reinforced concrete balcony front which has a rough or bush hammered finish. Each gallery seats seventy persons in six rows of tiered benches of similar design to those in the nave.

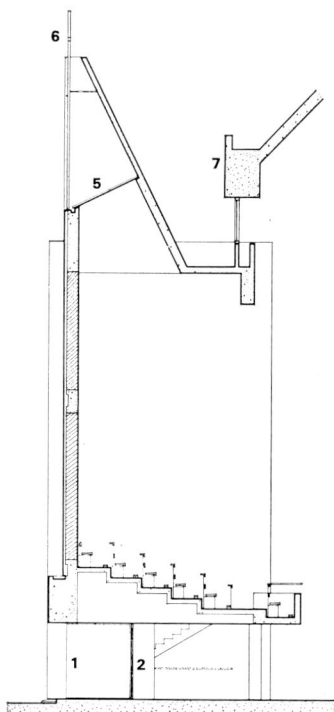

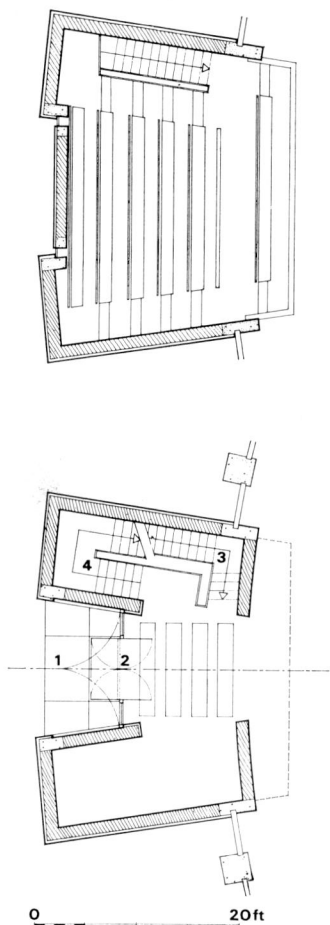

97. *Plan of gallery over porch*

98. *Far left: section of porch*

Key:
1. *Main doors*
2. *Inner glass screen*
3. *Stair from sacristies*
4. *Stair to gallery*
5. *Roof light*
6. *Bronze cross*
7. *Lower ring beam*

99. *Plan of porch at nave level*

0   20ft

136

14. THE BUILDING ORGANISATION

Cathedral building and industrialisation

Building construction is changing from craft to industrial production. It is inevitable that the machine will, in time, replace the hand in meeting the world-wide demand for shelter caused by the change from rural to industrial economy. This is not to say that ancient crafts like bricklaying, tiling and carpentry will die, for there will still be traditional construction for particular buildings; besides which there is the vast number of existing buildings which cannot be written off, and must be maintained and modernised as the need arises.

The demand for churches, still less cathedrals, is not so great that they will be purchased as mass-produced objects, as can be the case with housing. In any case, a church, having very special functions and being the focus of a wider scene, is expected to exhibit individualities in design which in, say, a block of flats, could be mere eccentricity. But this is not to say that expressionism is desirable in design – the originality of Sagrada Familia or Ronchamp may be a justification in their own terms but few architects have the divine inspiration of Gaudi or Le Corbusier and the pursuit of self-expression more often than not leads to mere novelty. Neither is it to say that churches should not be produced by industrialised processes: on the contrary, there is everything to be said for so doing.

Industrialisation means, of course, the abandonment of that reverence for hand craft in church building which was so successfully engendered by the arts and crafts movement. But, paradoxically, the acceptance of technology is a return to the true spirit of mediaeval building; at the sites of the great cathedrals were found not only the best brains and greatest skills but the most advanced tools and machines. By comparison, two great modern English cathedrals, Truro and Liverpool Anglican are, as structures, barren exercises in stylistic revival: it is the new constructions of the industrial revolution – railway stations, bridges, power stations and the like – that exhibit the adventurous attitude to construction which characterised mediaeval building.

It is now becoming apparent that, if the church is to provide the buildings it needs, there is neither the time nor the money for the luxury of ignoring scientific invention and the machine. The story of the building of the Metropolitan Cathedral is proof enough if proof be needed: Lutyens set his heart against modern technology and his building was constructed by a handful of craftsmen using only primitive machines, without a time and progress schedule, let alone a cost programme. Under those conditions it took some seven years to build the crypt and reach nave floor level. The new cathedral rejected the attitudes that made the crypt, embraced modern technology, and was able to shelter its two thousand congregation some four years after the contractor arrived on site.

Two broad types of building technology were adopted: the prefabrication of parts and the use of machines for their assembly and erection. The cathedral, being an individual non-repetitive design, was not, of course, built to any prefabricated system, and the degree to which the processes were industrialised was strictly defined by cost analysis and performance: if time could be saved and, along with it, money, then parts were prefabricated; but always subject to the over-riding consideration that a cathedral is expected to have a long life – prefabricated units set difficult problems of jointing which, on the exterior, can be critical.

I have already mentioned the prefabrication of components like the glass and concrete panels and the roofing units. The main structural frame, being built in-situ (that is, moulded in its final position) from the ground to the roof of the tower, was not a prefabricated structure; none the less, prefabrication took a large part in its construction: the formwork (or mould) into which the concrete was poured was made in a carpenter's shop, the steel falsework which supported the formwork was fabricated off the site, and the steel reinforcement was bent and assembled in units on the roof of the crypt before being placed in its position in the formwork.

There were, too, a large number of processes which, although not prefabrication, were far removed from traditional craft techniques: for example, the Portland stone on the individual buildings is not masonry construction built up block by block but a veneer of pre-cut slabs, cut to size by machine off the site and delivered for fixing when required.

Whether or not the parts were prefabricated, machines took a major part in their assembly and one of them, a great tower crane, so dominated the erection of the structure that all other operations were geared to it.

I was fortunate in having the experience of considerably larger contracts; in particular, Hinkley Point nuclear power station, built by a consortium and making use of the most advanced techniques available, to rigorous time and cost controls. Its success had depended on a group of scientists, engineers, architects and administrators having enough humility to be willing to bend their particular expertise in the interests of the total conception. It seemed to me that if, at Liverpool, we could forget the mystique surrounding traditional cathedral building and bring instead the attitudes that permeated the building of Hinkley Point, we would have the greatest possible chance of producing an efficient structure, in the quickest possible time and at the lowest possible cost. Accordingly, I talked to Cardinal Heenan and, to my joy and surprise (I did not know him then), he was enthusiastic, particularly about a five-year building period when he had been led to believe ten years would be needed.

Cost and time

The original competition design was to an absolute minimum cost and in its development better finishes, such as mosaic to the frame and Portland stone to the chapels, were introduced. The costs were controlled by a bill of quantities prepared by John Stoward of Franklin & Andrews, from which a contract figure of one and a half million pounds was negotiated

with the building contractor. During the building period there was a rise
in costs, due to new requirements like the tea room, unforeseen conditions,
such as the exceptionally deep foundations and, of course, to the national
increase in cost of labour and materials. The final figure was, in round
figures, £1,900,000.

Cost decisions were extraordinarily difficult to determine because of
the requirement for a building of long life with minimum maintenance
costs: thus, we tended to use expensive materials like stainless steel and
bronze because they require relatively little upkeep. It was just as difficult
to establish an economic time for erection. The estimated time was four
years but, if cost had not been a major factor, we could have done it more
quickly. For example, if the building was going to earn a large rent on its
completion, as is the case with a commercial office block on a site worth
hundreds of thousands of pounds, extra costs on saving time might well
have been justified. But a cathedral earns no revenue and the time was

determined as a function of cost: for example, had it been too fast, costs could have risen through the labour force working over-time or, conversely if too slow, money would have been wasted through expensive machines not being used to their maximum capacity. Four years appeared to be the economic period and that is, in fact, how long it took.

Organisation of the site

The average building site, with its holes in the ground, scaffolding, piles of assorted materials, sheds, mechanical equipment and apparent junk lying about, does not suggest that building construction is a rational process, let alone a highly organised one. And yet the work will have been planned just as the building itself has been planned.

At Liverpool our common technical approach to the construction made accurate planning of the site itself and all the operations that were to take place on it absolutely essential. Although the site was a large one, when the area of the actual building was taken away, comparatively little working space remained and, apart from the rectangular roof of the crypt, most of it was in narrow strips on the perimeter.

The drawing (101) shows how the site was planned. The tower crane was sited on the centre point of the cathedral, ultimately the position for the high altar, and its jib was long enough to cover the entire building and much of the site area surrounding it. So expensive a tool had to be kept in constant use and the whole programming of the cathedral over the major part of the constructional period depended on and was directly geared to its speed of operation. The site could well be considered as a number of factories, the products of which would be ultimately handled by the jib of the crane, operating like a giant hand from above.

All the concrete required for the construction was produced by a mixing plant close to the site entrance, for ease of access for heavy lorries. It was fed from large stores of aggregate and cement and controlled by a small office and site laboratory.

The steel reinforcement for the concrete was stored on the roof of the crypt, where it was bent and assembled in large sections for placing in position. A light railway track was run across the roof to bring the sections within reach of the crane.

A large proportion of concrete was precast, in order to reduce construction time and to avoid the difficulties of pouring concrete at great heights: this was done in a precasting yard next to the concrete mixing plant.

A third factory was the joiners' shop, which produced all the framework required for the in-situ concrete, including the main structural frame; other factories were set up to produce the composite nave roof panels and the pinnacles.

At the hub of all this activity were the site offices, next to the crypt. As has already been mentioned, precise and accurate planning of all stages of the work was essential. The occasional discussion between foremen about which job to tackle next was replaced by a critical path study, kept under constant review — a critical path is a form of time programme that selects the operations which are essential because delay in completing them means delay to all later operations; this chain of essential operations is known as the critical path, and the whole job must be governed by it.

Regular site meetings were used, not to discuss the virtues of materials or the details of construction, but to check the course of events against the critical path, to recognise well ahead the possible sources of delay and to eliminate them.

101. Plan showing the organisation of the building site

Key:
  1. *Tower crane*
  2. *Derrick crane*
  3. *Concrete mixing plant*
  4. *Steel reinforcement store*
  5. *Steel bending yard*
  6. *Light railway*
  7. *Precast concrete yard*
  8. *Roof panel factory*
  9. *Joinery shop*
  10. *Site offices*
  11. *Subcontractors' offices*
  12. *Electric sub-station*
  13. *Canteen*

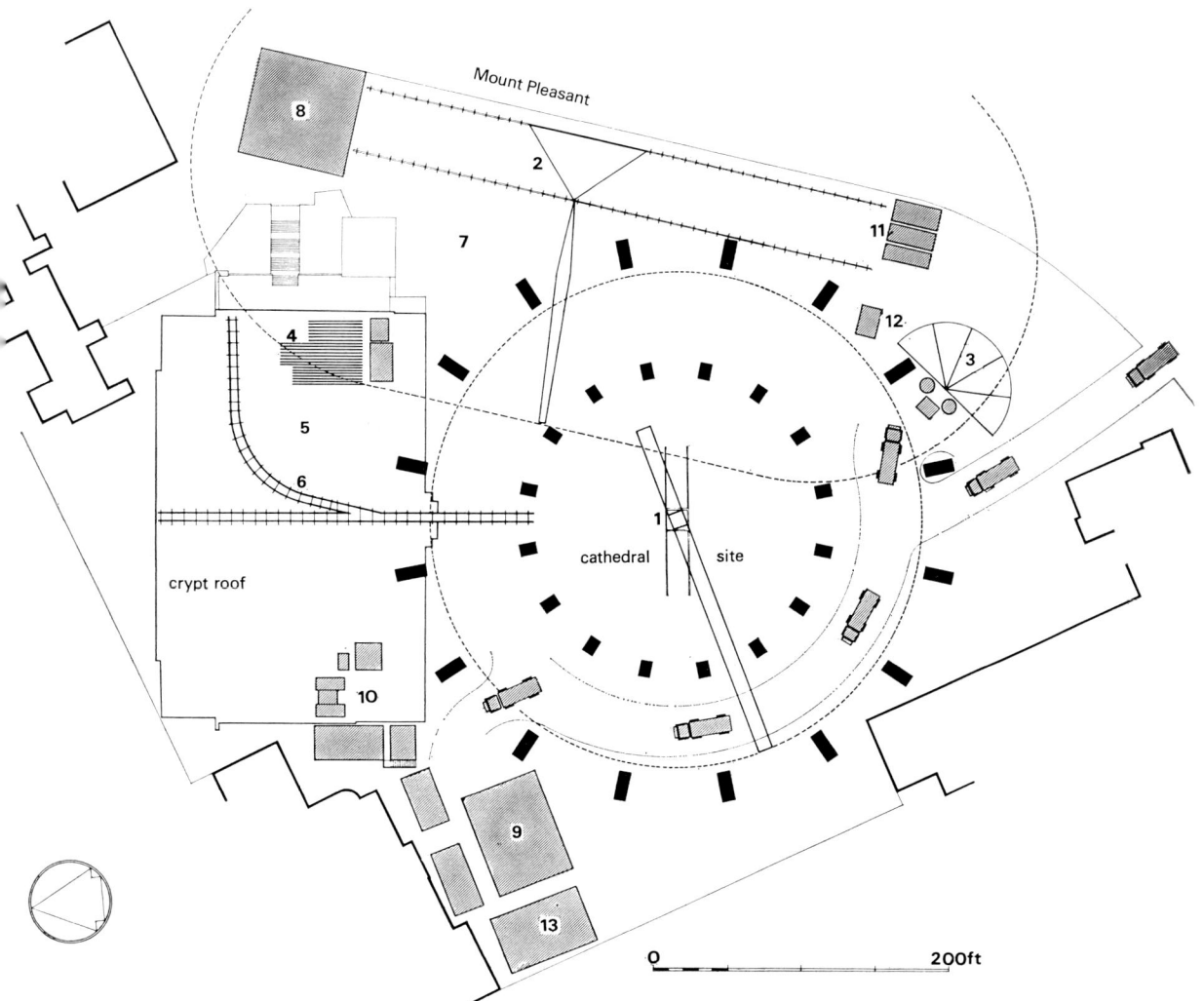

15. THE ERECTION

The tools

The tower crane, to which the whole process of erection was geared, is one of the most splendid and spectacular tools that man has yet invented for constructing buildings. Its use was recommended by the team who studied possible methods of erecting the building. The idea was to erect a crane in the centre of the building, with a very long jib which, moving through a complete circle, would cover the whole area of the circular nave; and that it should be capable of being extended well above the height of the tower, so that it could place the pinnacles in position – a difficult operation: at Coventry a helicopter was used to lift the spire.

The crane finally decided on was a Jules Weitz, specially made for the job at Lyons, France; it would lift four tons, had a radius of 164 feet and would rise to a total height of 320 feet – at that time the largest saddle-jib type of tower crane in the world. Only four of them had been previously produced, three of them being used at the Sydney Opera House.

Although costly, it was clear that the crane would pay for itself in the saving of labour, time and special falsework. There was an initial difficulty, in that the crane was going to take many months to manufacture and assemble and we needed to order it long before the contract was signed – only by having it at the very start of the job could the maximum work be extracted from so expensive a tool. I went to the Cathedral Committee and explained the dilemma we were in and asked them to order the crane with the knowledge that, if they did not go ahead with the contract, the crane would be theirs and, since they were unlikely to have any use for it, its disposal would cost them £30,000. They rose to the occasion: the crane arrived at Liverpool docks soon after construction began and was erected to become a spectacular and surprising element in Liverpool's topography – I had seen a tower crane hovering over the new gilt dome of the Dome of the Rock in Jerusalem but this was nothing like so spectacular as Liverpool's gaunt and immense structure growing out of the tower (100).

During the initial stages of building, the crane was mobile on a length of track; but, when the structure of the cathedral reached the main ring beam, the base of the crane was anchored down and its tower tied back to the structure of the building.

The skill of the driver and that of his banksman (who provided an extra pair of eyes at ground level), were of great importance for, had they made the slightest error in handling large elements like the precast roofing slabs and the concrete and glass panels, the slightest damage would have meant scrapping the complete unit and, of course, serious delay.

The building grew up round the crane until, eventually, it was almost completely embedded. The problem was then to get the crane down again; easy enough on an open site but here was the extraordinary, probably 142 unique, condition of the crane being embedded for its full height inside the building. Although this is not a book about building construction I cannot resist mentioning the ingenious way the crane was made to dismantle itself. First, the 77 ft. nose of the jib was disconnected and lowered from the remainder of the jib down to roof level, where it was taken over by the derrick crane. From then on everything had to be taken down through the inside of the building. The rest of the jib, ninety feet of it and weighing some ten tons, was pivoted from the top of the derrick until it hung vertically: it was then lowered through a hole in the tower roof down to the podium car park. Then followed, through the hole, other components until only the vertical tower was left, which dismantled itself section by section to ground level.

The tower crane had a servant in the form of a derrick crane to fetch and carry for it. This crane had a jib of 150 ft., capable of lifting five tons. It ran on rails between the concrete pre-casting yard, which itself had a mobile gantry, and the area of the actual building operations.

Unusual tools and equipment were invented to deal with special problems of the construction. Examples include a rubber-tyred buggy operated by air winch, to run up the 45° face of the buttresses and convey concrete and mortar needed during the fixing of the nave roof panels; and a rigid jig to both position and lift the stainless steel wind bracing within the lantern tower.

The erection sequence

The main structure was erected in four broad stages over a period of four years. The diagrams that follow were prepared by the contractor to show the main tasks and the sequence in which he intended to execute them. For the sake of clarity they show an over-simplified picture and, in actual practice, there was considerable overlapping between one operation and another, so that the different trades had a steady and continuous flow of work. However, the diagrams gave everyone concerned a clear mental picture of the broad tasks in front of us and the consulting engineer prepared more detailed diagrams of particular problems.

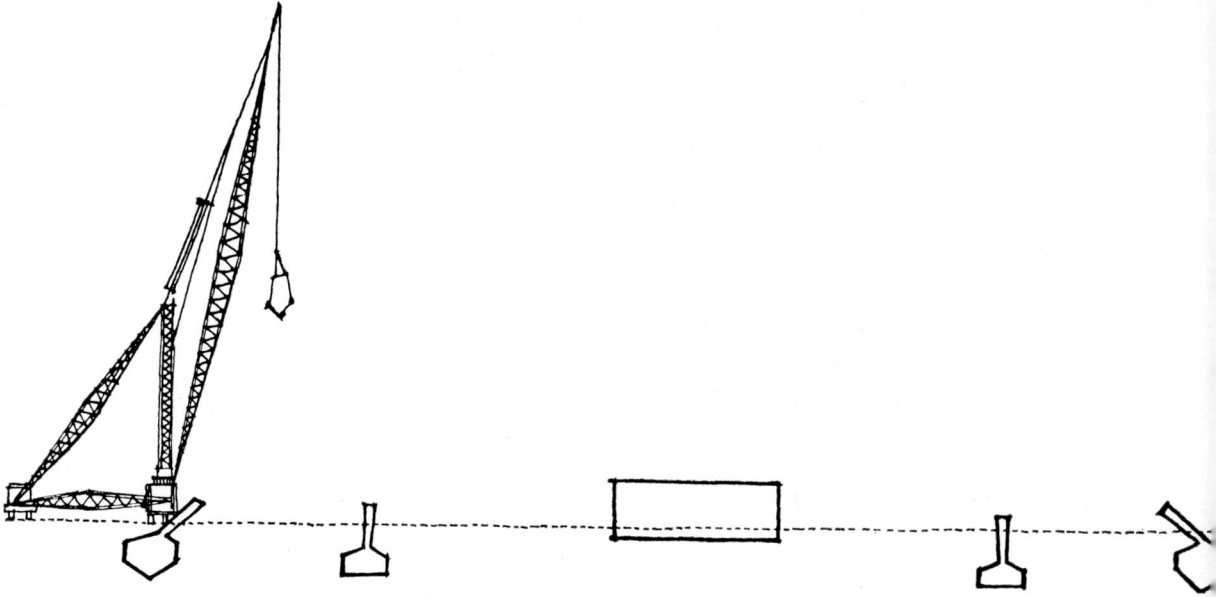

Stage 1: Foundations

The first stage of the construction is shown in (103). It consisted of setting out the site, erecting the contractors' plant and laying the foundations. The concrete foundations for the flying buttresses and vertical columns of the sixteen frames have been built. The derrick crane, on the left of the diagram, lifts the heavy loads but, in the centre of the structure, a solid block of concrete has been raised to the podium level, to take the tower crane: it is appropriate that the most important tool occupies the position of the most important object, for this block of concrete is also the foundation for the high altar.

The foundations were on rock and, in practice, there was nothing exceptional about them, until we came to excavating for the flying buttresses adjacent to the Lutyens crypt. Four of these had to penetrate the crypt foundations and, as there were no records, the structure had to be bored to discover what it was made of and how far down the excavations had to go to find a safe bottom. This was bad enough but, excavating for one of the holes, an old quarry road was found over an infilling of rubbish: so the digging had to go down to a depth of 90 ft. before solid rock was found: and that was, of course, at an angle of 45° – the rake of the buttresses. Specialists in underground exploration, like that required in coal mining, were called in to deal with the excavation and afterwards the hole was filled with mass concrete, itself a difficult structural problem. The whole process was, to the engineers, an exciting adventure in advanced civil engineering, to be shown to admiring visitors and photographed from every conceivable angle: my own enthusiasm was tempered by the thought of so much buried money.

102. *Facing page: foundations for the frame are laid, and also a concrete block reaching up to podium level, to support the tower crane and become the foundation for the High Altar*

103. *The site from the west. So far, all the work is out of sight below ground*

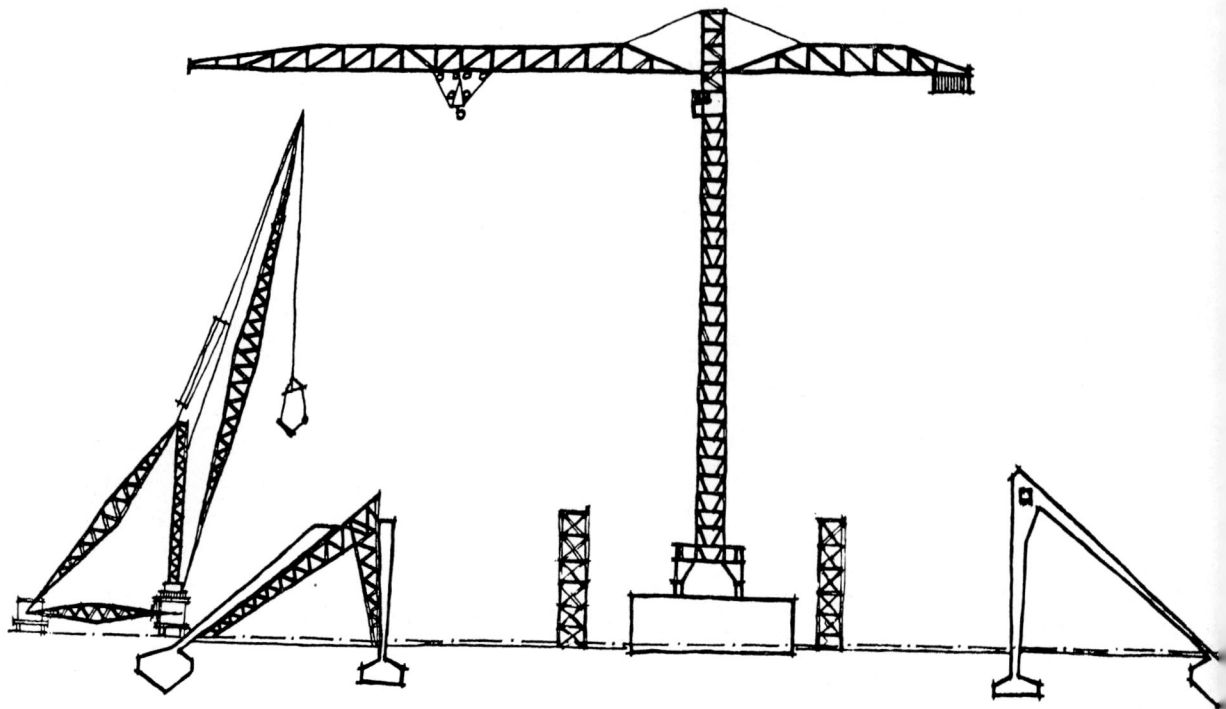

Stage 2: Nave frame

The second stage (105) is the construction of the frame of the nave, that is, from the foundations to the bottom of the conical roof. The tower crane now dominates the site and its chief task is pouring the concrete of the flying buttresses, the vertical columns and the lower ring beam which joins them together – shown on the right of the diagram. The steel false-work to support the structure is now a major feature; the columns are supported by pairs of lattice steel towers and the flying buttresses by raking steel trusses spanning from the ground to the top of the towers. In the centre of the picture steel lattice towers are being erected to support the main ring beam at the base of the tower.

As the structure was designed to be in compression, the erection sequence had to be devised to leave the building in a reasonable state of stress and strain: that is, the weight of the building and the load of the wind had to be taken down to the foundations over the whole structure as evenly as possible.

We were faced with one of the major problems of all large homogeneous concrete structures: shrinkage. This happens not because of the water drying out, although there is a minute shrinkage, but because the hydra-tion of the cement causes the concrete first to expand and then to contract. The lower ring beam, having a circumference of about six hundred feet, was particularly liable to undesirable stresses with changes of temperature.   146

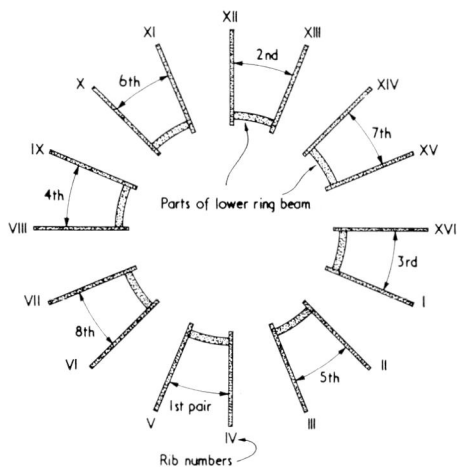

104. Facing page: the tower crane is in place; on the left a buttress and a column, partly completed, are supported by steel falsework. On the right is a similar unit, complete up to the lower ring beam

105. Above: another view from the west: sections of the lower ring beam have been completed

106. Plan showing the sequence of erection of the frames up to the same stage as (104)

For this reason, among others, the nave frames were erected in pairs connected by sections of the beam (106). The gaps between the pairs were then filled in with other sections of the ring beam, excepting four which were temporarily closed with steel beams, enabling movement to take place. After some weeks, when the whole frame had cooled down, the gaps were closed during a period of cold weather.

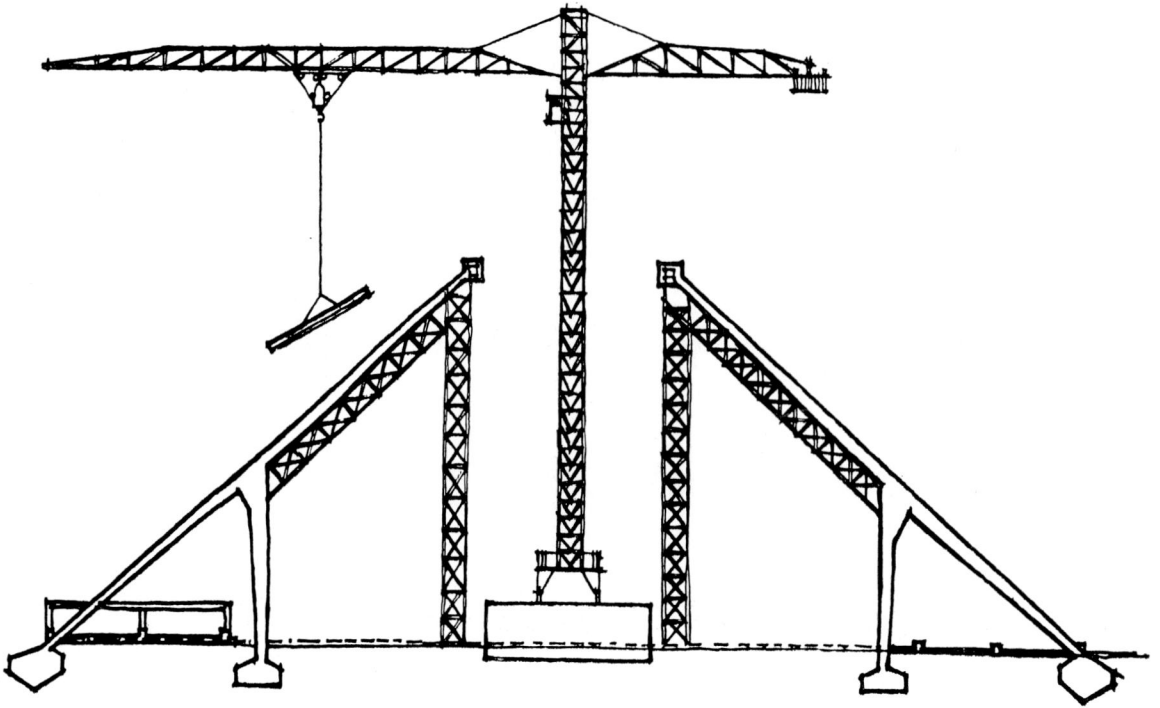

Stage 3: Conical roof

The third stage, shown in (108), is the construction of the conical roof – that is, from the lower ring beam to the main ring beam at the base of the tower. The central group of lattice trusses has been extended to the base of the tower, two short towers being adapted to make one tall one. The raking diagonal trusses have been taken down and re-fixed from the top of the nave frames to the top of the vertical towers, so that they can be re-used for supporting the sixteen ribs in the cone. In the diagram the crane is shown placing in position one of the prefabricated concrete beams or purlins which span between the frame to carry the pre-cast concrete roofing slabs. Work has begun on the foundations of the chapels and the construction of the podium has begun – on the left of the picture.

The casting of the roof cone and the main ring beam was just as intricate and difficult as the second stage. In order to spread the weight evenly throughout the whole of the structure, the concrete ribs and the beam were cast in pairs and in the sequence shown on the plan (109). The segments of the ring beam were cast concurrently with the ribs but gaps were left between them, the ring beam being supported by jacks; the sixteen joints were not made until after all shrinkage had taken place, a period of some six weeks. The lowering of the jacks was a momentous day for everyone on the site. The weight was transferred from the steel falsework to the structure itself which, for the first time, became self-supporting.

148

107. *Facing page: the nave frame complete: the falsework has been lifted to support the frame of the cone roof and upper ring beam*

108. *View from the northwest: the structure has risen as far as the upper ring beam. To the right is the bell tower.*

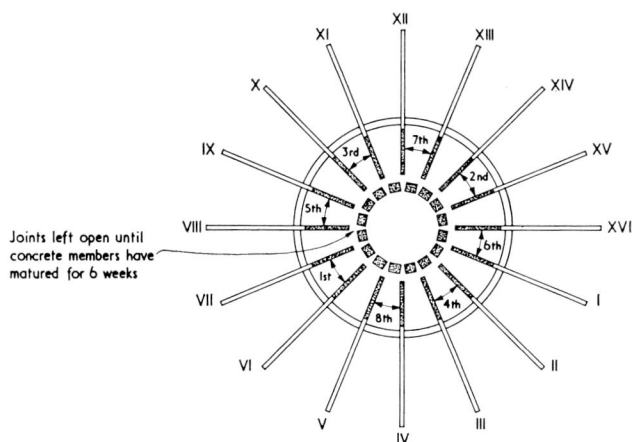

Joints left open until concrete members have matured for 6 weeks

109. *Plan showing sequence of erection of ribs for cone roof, up to the same stage as (107)*

149

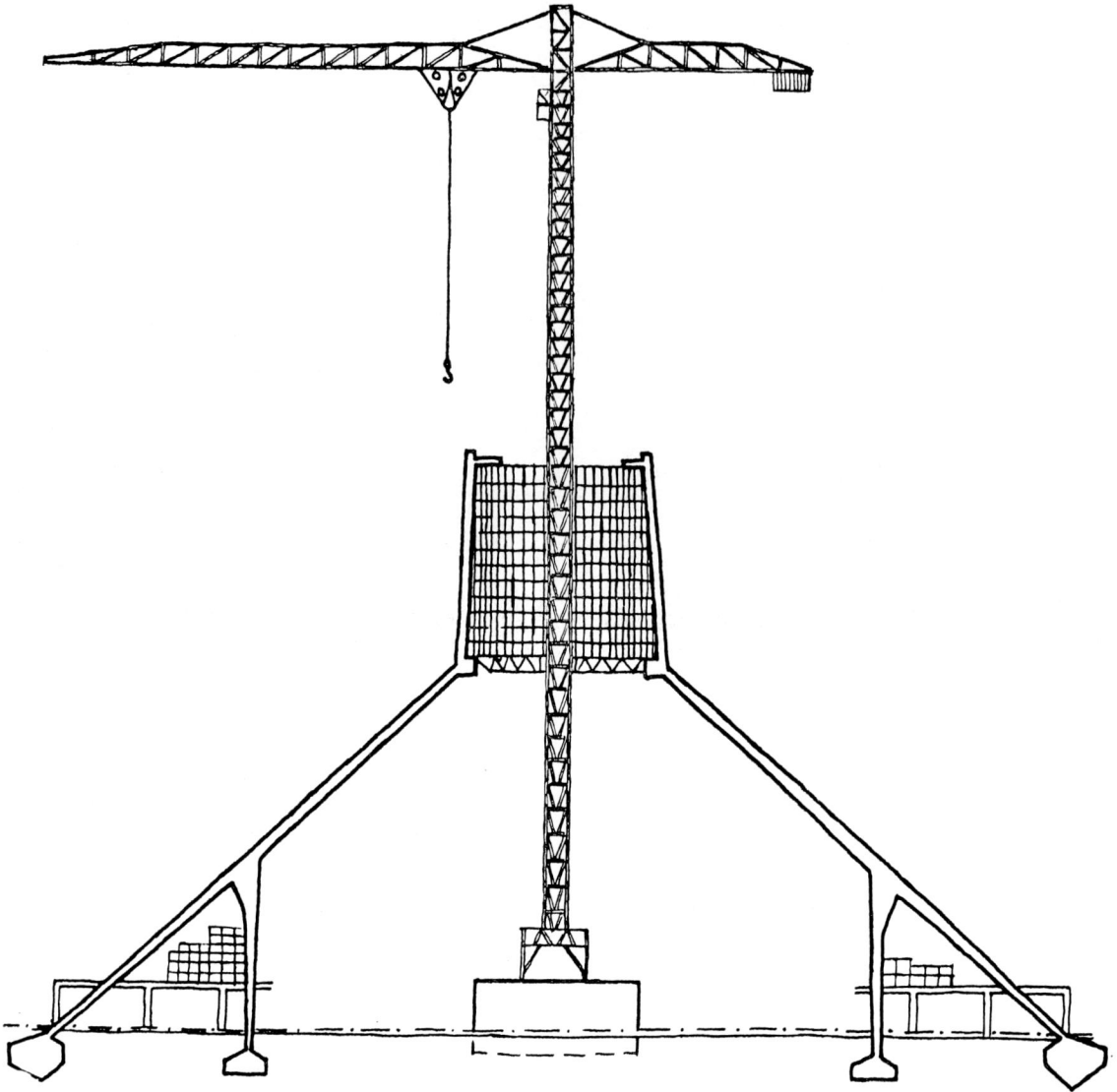

Stage 4: Tower

The fourth stage, (III), is the construction of the tower. The building is now a self-supporting cage, the steel falsework having been dismantled. The tower crane is raised to its limit of 300 ft. and is braced against the main ring beam. The nave has been sealed off at the top of the roof by a temporary floor to provide a new working level and allow work to proceed underneath – speedy access was provided by a temporary lift, summoned by hitting its framework with an iron bar. The sixteen ribs of the main frame are being concreted, after which the precast concrete and glass panels will be lifted by the crane and bolted to the frame. The final tasks on the structural shell will be the construction of the roof dome and lifting the pinnacles into position.

110. *Facing page:*
the crane fully extended
to complete the tower

111. *View from the south. While work proceeds on the tower, the chapels*
begin to rise. When the tower was complete, the crane dismantled itself
through two holes in the tower roof: their position can be traced in air
view (10)

After these four stages had been completed all that remained was the completion of the chapels, the nave floor and the services. This we planned to complete by January 1967, leaving some four months for installing special equipment like the seating and the works of art. This is more or less what we did; each of the five stages provided a landmark in the evolution of the cathedral but, in spite of the great experience and organising skill of the contractor, we had a mad scramble to finish in time for the consecration. It was not the installation of special equipment, extra to the building contract, that caused the delays, although it was a contributory factor; it was the unreliability of Liverpool building labour.

151

16. THE CATHEDRAL BUILDERS

It is the intention in this, the last chapter, to give some idea of the extra-ordinary diversity of skill and talents that are drawn into the making of a large building. It is the intention, too, to place on record the names of those who, over the years, have in one way or another, been involved in its creation; both to give them their due and to correct the inevitable bias of a book primarily concerned with architectural design.

But this is not a record of all those who have made the cathedral. How could it be? For without the will of the many thousands of people, both inside the Catholic diocese and out, nothing at all could have happened on Brownlow Hill. It is only through their efforts and sacrifices and through the devotion of servants of the church like Monsignor Turner (who, dur-ing the last thirty-one years, has raised two million pounds), that we in the building trade could come together and make the cathedral.

The historical background

The first Liverpool Cathedral was commissioned by Dr. Alexander Goss, Bishop of Liverpool 1856–1870, who entrusted the design to Edward Welby Pugin, son of the great Augustus. His neo-Gothic design was dedicated to St. Edward and was to be in the grounds of St. Edward's College, Everton. Owing to pressure on funds for churches and schools for the rapidly expanding Irish population the project was abandoned after the Lady Chapel had been built – it is now known as the Church of Our Lady Immaculate, St. Domingo Road.

In 1911 Pope Pius X divided England into three provinces of West-minster, Birmingham and Liverpool. Dr. Whiteside was the first Arch-bishop of the north and his successor, Archbishop Keating, revived the idea of building a cathedral as a memorial to Dr. Whiteside. He was responsible for starting a fund in 1922 and, by the time he died six years later, £122,000 had been raised and negotiations were in progress for the Brownlow Hill site which was then a vacant workhouse.

Archbishop Keating's successor, Archbishop Downey, commissioned Sir Edwin Lutyens to design the new cathedral and, in 1930, secured the site for £100,000. Lutyens' first design was for a cathedral to seat 10,000, at an estimated cost of £3,000,000 and the time for building was put at a minimum of twenty years. The building of the crypt was begun in 1934 and it was almost completed by 1940, when the war stopped all work.

After Lutyens' death in 1944, Adrian Gilbert Scott was appointed to execute the original design. But in 1952 the estimate of cost had risen to £27,000,000 and so Scott was asked to produce a revised design using the crypt as the base. His design reduced the cost to £4,000,000 but it was received by architectural critics without enthusiasm.

In 1957 Dr. (now Cardinal) Heenan acceded as fifth Archbishop. He decided that all building work must stop on the completion of the crypt (it was opened in October 1958) and that an open competition should be held for an entirely new design.

The competition and the assessors

The actual design for the cathedral began with the Building Committee and the assessors, Cardinal Heenan, Sir Basil Spence and Mr. David Stokes, writing the brief for the competition.

The competition was open to any architect who was a British subject and some thousand people sent for the competition conditions after their publication in October 1959. My interest in the competition was, at first, curiosity but I became impressed by the open nature of the conditions and the very unusual problems they posed. Working alone, I produced a broad design, primarily as a mental exercise and then, a month before the final date, decided to submit it, to see how I stood in relationship to other competitors. I borrowed staff who could be spared from other jobs and we shut ourselves up and drew out the final drawings. Felix Darnell, now in practice in Israel, understudied me and the rest of a cosmopolitan group included William Ainsworth, Brian Bagot, Frank Heaversedge, who has since returned to his native Rhodesia, Edouardo Orrego, now a member of the Peruvian Government and Stephen Kapos, who came to us from Hungary.

The designs were anonymous; 298 competitors submitted schemes and No. 253, which was mine, was declared the winner, a disconcerting experience which was relieved by Cardinal Heenan remarking, "I know what I would say, Mr. Gibberd, I would say, 'Thank God'."

Although, on the face of it, there were two parties to the competition, the assessors and the competing architects, other specialists were involved. The assessors consulted Messrs. Reynolds & Young, the quantity surveyors, to check the costs and Ove Arup, the consulting engineer, to advise on the feasibility of the structural solutions; incidentally, had they not done so, I might not have won, for imaginative designs were eliminated for being impracticable, or far in excess of the cost limit. I, on my part, discussed the structure with James Lowe, the consulting engineer and John Stoward, the quantity surveyor, estimated the cost – when I telephoned him to ask him to do this, subject, of course, to it being less than one million pounds, he complained he had already done six others.

The client or cathedral committee

After the competition, Archbishop Heenan and the Cathedral Committee, which he chaired, were my clients.

For the first eighteen months they were completely involved in the development of the design (models and explanatory drawings were used to make my intentions crystal clear) and afterwards their agreement was sought on every major decision.

K.   G.L.C

The members of the Cathedral Committee in September 1960 were:

The Most Revd. J. C. Heenan, DD, PH.D., Archbishop of Liverpool (Chairman)

Rt. Revd. Mgr. Canon Thomas Adamson, VG

Rt. Revd. Mgr. Canon Thomas A. Turner

Very Revd. Canon Walter Grace

Very Revd. Canon Michael J. O'Sullivan

Very Revd. Albert Bentley, PH.D., MA

J. J. Williams, Esq.

T. E. Hall, Esq, ARIBA

Very Revd. Canon Arthur G. Maguire (Hon. Sec. and Joint Hon. Treasurer)

Very Revd. Mgr. T. G. McKenna, who succeeded the last-named as Hon. Sec.

Further Committee members, appointed at later dates, were:

Revd. Thomas P. Marsh, PH.D.

Revd. Richard R. Wright, OSB, MA

Revd. Joseph Gibb

T. J. C. Taylor, Esq. LL B.

Very Revd. Mgr. Cyril Taylor

Archbishop Beck succeeded Archbishop Heenan in March, 1964, and, during the former's illness in 1967, Auxiliary Bishop Harris acted for him.

Monsignor McKenna, the Cathedral Administrator, was our chief link with the Cathedral Committee from the early development of the design until the completion of the contract – he even attended the monthly site meetings.

Professional groups

I possess a photograph of the architect inspecting the building of the Albert Memorial in Kensington, in morning coat and top hat, with the builder and foreman in respectful attendance – the splendid professional protecting his client's interests from the worldly tradesmen. The scene is ludicrous compared with a site meeting today, where it would not be unusual to find thirty highly-qualified specialists hammering out the construction problems as a team. Team work penetrates the complete operation, which is not to say that it is implemented by a series of committees – individuals dominate particular teams – and, in the case of a building which makes great demands on aesthetic experience (of which the cathedral is the most demanding), one individual, the architect, carries the ultimate responsibility.

Three professional groups were formed immediately the competition was won: architects, engineers and quantity surveyors.

My partner, J. B. Forrest, was responsible for conducting the whole project, from the preparation of the working drawings to the final completion of the job. A large number of architectural assistants worked with him, of whom the principals were John Berreen, Gerald Elves, Elizabeth

Hogan and Teresa Whitmarsh-Everiss; such respect and admiration existed between the last-named and my partner that she is now Mrs. Forrest. The Clerk of Works responsible to us for the satisfactory execution of the building work was John Tiernan, whose devotion to the cathedral began with Lutyens and the building of the crypt. During the last two years, when the job was complicated by so many skills and so much special equipment, Philip Harrison acted as site architect.

The consulting engineers were Lowe & Rodin. James Lowe was intimately involved in the structure from the competition drawings on-wards. His partner, Jack Rodin, assisted during design and controlled the structural analyses and Lionel Essers was resident engineer on the site.

The quantity surveyors were Franklin & Andrews. John Stoward, the partner in charge, gave me the original competition estimate and he personally negotiated the contract. His key people were his associate, Roy Woodward, assisted by Colin Rice, on pre-contract work; and his associate, Jack Evans, assisted by Len Crossley, on post-contract work.

In the early stages of this development the work was dominated by the architects, structural engineers and quantity surveyors but, as the problems were studied in greater depth, other professions became involved.

I have already discussed the work of the acoustic consultants, Humphreys & Creighton. Together they took sole responsibility; the only assistance they had was from Mrs. Humphreys, who fired a revolver in the nave when the acoustics were being tested.

Of the two main services, mechanical and electrical installations, the former was designed by Young, Austen & Young, Ltd. They had already installed the heating in the Lutyens crypt and they both designed and installed that for the cathedral. Our first discussions were with E. Austen and subsequent ones were with Dai Davies who, with E. Bull, also super-vised the work on site.

The electrical consultants were Barlow, Leslie & Partners and J. W. J. Leslie was personally responsible for the design, assisted by Barry Johnson-Smith and, latterly, by Peter Sandford.

The main contractor

It was not very long before it became apparent that we had a missing technician, the building contractor. Had the design been a conventional one, we could have completed the work and invited competitive tenders. As it was, there was little precedent for much of the construction; in particular, the structural frame was a special hazard, for large sums of money could be involved in the scaffolding falsework and machines with which to construct it. I explained our dilemma to the Cathedral Committee and they at once agreed that we could appoint a contractor, with the intention of giving him the job when it had been finally worked out – providing, of course, his price was reasonable.

The consulting engineer, quantity surveyor and my office looked for a contractor with exceptional organising skill and technical expertise. It mattered little whether or not he had a single craftsman on his payroll. 155

Our choice was finally reduced, after discussions between us, to three large firms, each with different experience and character but all capable of tackling an immense and unique constructional problem. They were given the design as far as it had then evolved and invited to write a brief report on how they would set about building the job.

Each contractor was invited to discuss his report with us and we eventually recommended that Taylor Woodrow Construction Ltd. should be appointed. I had, metaphorically speaking, a hot line with A. J. Hill, the Chairman, and the Joint Managing Director in charge of the contract was Tom Reeves.

Occasional informal discussion quickly developed into daily consultations at all levels between those engaged on the job and we were fortunate indeed that J. F. Wilson, who was to become the project manager on site and his second in command, J. H. Baines, were both available for some months before the work actually started.

After two years, at the end of the purely structural work, J. F. Wilson was succeeded by Peter Stewart, who carried the job through to completion, assisted by David Taylor and Derek Shepherd.

Through the whole construction period, the general foreman on the site was Tom McNulty.

Research and development groups

Due to the lack of precedent for so much of the construction, use was made of scientific research and development available to the building industry.

The Building Research Station near Watford has done more serious research than any other body into the nature and behaviour of building materials and it was inevitable that we should consult them. The consulting engineer discussed a number of problems with Dr. Bate, Dr. Nurse and A. J. Newman and we sought advice on the behaviour of many materials from them and from such specialist organisations as the Lead Development Association, as well as from subcontractors and suppliers of all kinds.

As I mentioned when discussing the structure,* a large model in fine concrete was made of the frame and tested by the Cement and Concrete Association at Wexham Springs, under Dr. R. E. Rowe – a spectacular experiment in which the equivalent of a Boeing 707 was driven into the tower and one, moreover, which produced considerable publicity, such is the attraction of novelty. Tests were also made at the National Physical Laboratory under the direction of C. Scruton, where a model was placed in a wind tunnel to check the load imposed on the building by the wind at any given velocity.

Advice on the epoxy resin used for the lantern and nave glass was given to the engineers by Shell Chemicals Limited and some of the testing was done by Shell at their laboratories at Egham. Further advice was given to Patrick Reyntiens by Arthur Letts of Beck-Koller Limited, the suppliers, and more tests were made at Reyntiens' studio.

* Page 52.

The development of the design for the nave roof, covered with aluminium, necessitated a major research programme. The engineers and ourselves were advised by the Non-Ferrous Metals Association, S. G. Clements of British Aluminium Company Limited and J. McGilley of Frederick Braby and Company Limited. The National Polymer Research Institute advised on the synthetic resin that secured the aluminium in position and provided the insulation. T. T. Healy of the National College of Rubber Technology gave the background on resins and drew up performance specifications. Completed sections of the roof were tested by the Yarsley Testing Laboratories Limited. Advice on the pinnacles was given by David Powell of Polyplan Limited.

Subcontractors and suppliers

Modern building is so complex and specialised that a very large number of firms become involved in its execution. They can be broadly divided into subcontractors who are nominated by the architect with the client's approval; subcontractors appointed by the main contractor; and the suppliers of building materials and special equipment.

The cathedral required furnishings and equipment like an organ and bells, which are not found in a normal building: these did not form part of the building contract proper but were ordered through my office on behalf of the Cathedral Committee.

So many firms made a contribution to the building of the cathedral and their responsibilities were so diverse that I cannot do more than set them out below in alphabetical order. This is undoubtedly summary treatment for such effort and skill but the end product is there for all to see on Brownlow Hill. Whether it is fine architecture I do not know: what I do know is that it is both well built and economically built.

List of principal sub-contractors and suppliers

ALUMINIUM
Frederick Braby and Company Limited
The British Aluminium Company Limited

ARCHITECTURAL METAL WORK
Air Distribution Equipment Limited
Bigwood Brothers (Birmingham) Limited
A. Edmonds and Company Limited
S. W. Farmer and Son Limited
Gardiner Sons and Company Limited
Grundy Arnatt Limited
Hayes and Finch Limited
Hurst Franklin and Company Limited
D. J. Williams and Son Limited

ASPHALT AND TARMACADAM
General Asphalt Company (N.W. Counties) Limited

BELLS
Whitechapel Bell Foundry

BRICKS
The London Brick Company Limited

BUILDERS' HARDWARE
Abbey Building Supplies Company
Allied Ironfounders Limited
Alma Aluminium, Brass and Pattern Making Foundry
Arthur Beale Limited
J. D. Beardmore and Company Limited
British Ropes Limited
Cable Covers Limited
Samuel Fox and Company Limited
General Construction and Engineering Company Limited
Harris and Edgar Limited
Head Braiding Limited
Alfred Horrocks Limited
King and Company Limited
Langley (London) Limited
McWenney, Smallman and Company Limited
Rope and Marine Services Limited
Stracey Wheeler Limited
W. M. G. (Guildford) 1961 Limited
Arnold Wragg (Bolts and Nuts) Limited

BUILDERS' MERCHANTS' ITEMS
C. H. Harvey and Son Limited
Joseph Parr Limited

CATERING EQUIPMENT
Benham and Sons Limited

CHIMNEY POTS
Red Bank Manufacturing Company Limited

CONCRETE MATERIALS
Amalgamated Roadstone Corporation Limited
G.K.N. Reinforcements Limited
John Henshall (Quarries) Limited
McCall and Company Limited
ReadyMixed Concrete Limited
Ribblesdale Cement Limited

DEMOLITION
R. Young and Company Limited

DOOR MATS
Catholic Blind Institute

ECCLESIASTICAL METALWORK
F. Osborne and Company Limited
Wakely and Wheeler Limited

ELECTRICAL EQUIPMENT
Associated Electrical Industries Limited
Atlas Lighting Limited
Lumitron Limited
Merchant Adventurers Limited
Wandsworth Electrical Manufacturing Company Limited

ELECTRICAL INSTALLATION
Barlow and Young Limited

ENGINEERING SERVICES
Babcock and Wilcox Limited
Ground Engineering Limited

FIRE EXTINGUISHER EQUIPMENT
Foamite Limited
George Angus and Company Limited

FLOOR FINISHES
Art Pavements and Decorations Limited
Campbell and McDowd Limited
R. A. Davison and Company Limited
Diespeker and Company Limited
J. A. Hewetson and Company Limited
Kendall and Williams Limited
Marley Tile Company Limited
Rowan and Boden Limited

GLAZING, INCLUDING COLOURED GLASS
John Hardman and Company Limited
L. Keizer and Company Limited
Modern Art Glass Company Limited
J. G. Nicholls (1935) Limited

HEATING AND VENTILATION INSTALLATION
Young Austen and Young Limited

HOLY WATER STOUP BOWLS
S.G.B. (Dudley) Limited

INSULATION
Celcon Limited
Newalls Insulation and Chemical Company Limited
Turners Asbestos Cement Company Limited

IRONMONGERY
Alpha Architectural Ironmongery Limited
E. Hill Aldam and Company Limited
London Electric Firm Limited

JOINERY
A. W. Ambery Joinery Limited
Beresford and Hicks Limited
T. Blundell Limited
D. Burkle and Son Limited

David Powell Designs
John Sadd and Sons Limited
William Thornton and Sons Limited
Tysons (Joinery) Limited

LANDSCAPING
Claphams Nurseries Limited

LIFT INSTALLATION
Otis Elevator Company Limited

LIGHTENING PROTECTION
R. C. Cutting and Company Limited

MAINTENANCE EQUIPMENT AND STEEPLEJACKS
Access Equipment Limited
Brunswick Restoration Company Limited
Interior and Structural Cleaners Limited
Palmers Travelling Cradle and Scaffold Company Limited

MARBLE AND STONEWORK
Stone Masonry (North Western) Limited

MASTICS AND SEALANTS
Beck, Koller and Company (England) Limited
Evomastics Limited
May, Gurney and Company Limited
Servicised Limited
Tretol Limited

METAL DOORS
Bolton Gate Company Limited
Dreadnought Fireproof Doors (1930) Limited

MOSAIC
Proctor Lavender Mosaics Limited

ORGAN
J. W. Walker and Sons Limited

PAINT AND PAINTING
Cementone Limited
Henry Clarke and Sons Limited
Imperial Chemical Industries Limited
Sanders Pine Industrial Contractors Limited

PILING AND DEEP EXCAVATION
Cementation Company Limited
M and H Mining Contractors Limited

PLASTERING AND RENDERING
Expanded Metal Company Limited
Merseyside Plasterers Limited
Pollock Brothers (Liverpool) Limited
Whitley Moran and Company Limited

PLASTICS
William J. Cox Limited

Flexo Plastic Industries Limited
Instalrite Plastic Industries Limited
Polyplan Limited

PLUMBING AND DRAINAGE WORK
A. Dillon and Company Limited
G. N. Haden and Sons Limited

PRE-CAST CONCRETE
Ferroconcrete (Lancashire) Limited
Pencrete Limited
Tarmac Vinculum Limited
Trafford Concrete Products Limited
Trent and Hoveringham Concrete Companies Limited

ROOFLIGHTS
R. Seddon and Sons (St. Helens) Limited

SAFES
Chubb and Son's Lock and Safe Company Limited

SANITARY WARE
Adamsez Limited
Dent and Hellyer Limited

SCAFFOLDING
Mills Scaffold Company Limited

SIGNS
The Lettering Centre

SILK WALL HANGINGS
Lenygon and Morant Limited

SOUND REINFORCEMENT EQUIPMENT
Standard Telephones and Cables Limited

STONE AND SLATE
Dinorwic Slate Quarries Company Limited
Heys (Britannia) Quarries Limited
George Lindley and Sons Limited
Stone Firms Limited

STRUCTURAL STEEL
Bowman and Beddows Limited
George Lowe and Sons Limited
South Durham Steel and Iron Company Limited

WINDOW FRAMES AND PATENT GLAZING
Henry Hope and Sons Limited
Mellowes and Company Limited
Williams and Watson Limited